Poetry From
Southern England

Edited by Heather Killingray

First published in Great Britain in 2007 by:
Forward Press Ltd.
Remus House
Coltsfoot Drive
Peterborough
PE2 9JX
Telephone: 01733 898101
Website: www.forwardpress.co.uk

SB ISBN 1 84418 456 0

Foreword

Forward Press was established in 1989 to provide a platform for poets to showcase their works. Today, Forward Press continues to provide an outlet for new and established poets and *Poetry From Southern England* is tribute to this.

Poetry should be interesting and, above all else, accessible to all. Forward Press publications are for all lovers of traditional verse and of the art of rhyme, as well as for those who enjoy contemporary verse. *Poetry From Southern England* showcases both styles ensuring a varied read, and proving traditional and modern do complement each other.

Poetry From Southern England proudly showcases the region's best poets and the joy and inspiration we can all draw from where we live.

Contents

The Poems

Brixham Breakwater

This picture catches the light of gloaming
Of the fleeting joy, on a summer's evening.
The fisherman stands and baits the hook
Of the fishing rod, on Breakwater Beach.

Is he hoping to catch some cod or bream?
Or is it all only a dream?
To take some fish home, for tomorrow's dinner
Or even for breakfast, it could be a winner.

In the glow of the evening, of sunset pink
Would all the fish, do you think, be hoodwinked
To come and have, a tasty morsel, before
The Basking Shark, takes a mouthful?

Hopefully, he stays out at sea, for
He will not bother you or me, and
Leaves the fisherman to enjoy the night
That brings content, in the evening light.

Rosemary Peach (Torquay)

Receiver Of Wrecks

Tears flow for the Sei whale
Washed ashore, rock-stranded
Off Falmouth Bay.
He gasps in dry agony,
Sun-scorched.

Compassionate humans try to sustain him
With cooling slashes.
And in the Bay, his sad mate
Laments;
Helpless and grieving
She longs to be near.

Overnight he dies.

And his death is reported
To the Receiver of Wrecks.

Molly Campbell (Newton Abbot)

Kingfisher

Today I saw a kingfisher, I saw a kingfisher today
For one brief moment, azure and red gold
Caught and held my gaze, then he was gone!
I've walked beside this river many times before,
The muddy pathway squelching at my feet.
The February drabs and duns mingle with the greyness of the sky
The clay-brown stream, in spate, goes rushing by.

Today I saw a kingfisher, perched on a twig below the old stone bridge!
I froze, leaning upon the moss-encrusted parapet,
Staring in wonder for a single heartbeat's pause,
Then watched him fly away downstream.
I stood light-headed with surprise, thrilled at the sight
No vision of phoenix or a bird of paradise,
Could fill me with more pleasure or delight.

Today I saw a kingfisher, 'my favourite bird' I'd say,
Although I'd never seen one, that is not until today.
His image, popular in oil or watercolour,
Cannot compare with one brief sighting in reality,
But now I know for sure, that he is not a myth,
Oh bright elusive bird, spirit from another world,
I am honoured you revealed yourself, to me.

Today I saw a kingfisher, a fleeting vibrant spark,
Brilliant orange, rich and warm as flame,
Vivid blue, the ultimate and bluest of all blues,
Contrasting sharply with sad winter's dreary hues,
At home, I write upon my calendar 'KF',
To mark this day, most surely a red letter day
A kingfisher blue and orange day,
Today I saw a kingfisher, I saw a kingfisher today.

P M Parr (Launceston)

On Retiring To Sidmouth

I feel the wind,
I smell the sea,
Around me stretch
The hills serene.
I know this is
Enough for me.
No matter now
What might have been.

Evelyn Watson (Sidmouth)

The Village Show

There's ice cream and lollipops and rides on a train,
The sun's shining brightly - there's no sign of rain,
Ah, here comes our vicar to join in the fun
With one or two prizes he's already won!

There's book stalls and plant stalls and bright bric-a-brac
Collected by Miriam, and Trevor and Jack
The band is a-playin', the dancers a-dance;
That's old Mrs Brown there - she's just back from France!

And here to one side stands the great big marquee,
Let's just pop inside there before we have tea,
Ripe fruits and bright flowers quite dazzle our eyes,
Just look at those carrots - bet they'll win a prize!

The folks all have gathered, the young and the old,
With many warm greetings, and tales to be told
Of what they have seen there, and what they have done,
And how, once again, it has all been such fun!

Eileen Mellor (Taunton)

Winter Fairies

With tiniest, tiniest
fluttering wings
winter fairies
love to sing,
they land upon
a holly bush
with berries
red and bright,
they then, see someone
watching them
so to the skies
take flight.

To a peaceful stream
they'll fly away
to land and watch
some wildfowl play,
winter fairies
love to dance
when no one's
there to see,
as one little fairy
huffs and puffs
so cold and
unfit is she!

Winter fairies
love woodland ways
hiding in trees
that swing and sway,
they do keep watch
throughout the land
where a line of
elm trees, proudly stand.

In your garden
you may have docks
or maybe, somewhere
some old loose rocks
where winter fairies
inside will sleep
and if you're quiet
can take a peep!

Mary Ann Pont (Stoford, Salisbury)

Sounds Of Silence

I was born to silence of a different time
But for the clack of pendulum swing in a glass-fronted case
                                        of sombre style
Still corridors, just tap of leather heel on neat chess-chequered tile.
Gentle swish of tap in lime-washed outhouse sink
Earth hid stones on which the heavy-handled fork and spade will clink
The scrape of terracotta jars on stone-flagged floor
Faint rustle of dried herbs bunched and hung on pantry door
Moth wing flap of guttering candle flame about to die
A clutch of ornate chimney pots where playful winds moan and sigh
Creak and crunch on gravel of turning hoop-bound wooden wheel
And hobnailed scuff of trudging labourer, steel shod on sole and heel
Milk churn clang and solid clunk of latch-engaging, sagging
                                        wooden gate
Night owl sounds out it's getting late
The sounds of yesteryear.

Peter A Colenutt (Bristol)

Where Have They Gone?

Visitors arrive in all shapes and sizes
Young and old toward beaches advancing.
Remember the sun lotion, do not sizzle
A holiday here you should be enjoying.

But if it should rain, oh dear I will see
The cafes all full, no room for me.
Then to the shops like a stampede
Fighting for bargains, please watch my feet.

Now they are lost, can I tell them the way
To a hotel whose name they've forgotten?
The children are tired and not at all happy,
Somehow we manage, Mum and Dad thankful.

Today it is quiet, where have they gone?
The children I know are all back to school.
The families left, but oldies remain
Their memories worse, here I go again.

The locals all grumble at this yearly invasion
But where would I be with no conversation?
I think if I journey, perhaps go astray
A kind soul will help and not pass me by.

Freda Symonds (Torquay)

Vaughan Williams - English Composer

His music might rise suddenly
through high-arched naves
or sigh in the tall-spread trees
that march along the Roman roads,
wind from the green tracery
of thick and ancient woods
across calm, settled fields
long lived by.

He seems yet to stand in the evening,
his work well done,
on the rim of a venerable English hill
watching the whole island
spread out towards the west,
pervading what has gone,
translating it to music.

For he, like some ancient Druid bard,
has plucked intelligence,
not merely taught, but felt
in antique trees and secret glades,
and sends it out so surely
note by note
upon a timeless upward-spiralling journey.

Pam Redmond (Taunton)

The Village Church

The mellow ochre stone that
Medieval masons did hone
Ancient trees big and bold
Gnarled, inert and old
The elements that snapped and twisted the bough
Like broken outstretched arms now
Green grassy fields with kissing gates
That Sunday worshippers mingle through in reverent tête à têtes
Guardians of your church - hold your heads up high
Take pride in its simple Saxon beauty
That only the soulless could deny
English - so very English in Luckington's heart
This scene my city dweller's self is loath to part
One day I will walk this leafy lane,
To gaze in admiration at St Mary's and St Ethelbert's again.

Anita Hopes (Bristol)

Walking A Pet Dog In Suburbia

A quiet, empty, suburban street,
Gaily painted houses with gardens terribly neat,
Sam, a golden retriever, lives and roams
In one of these spotless suburban homes.

Walking a bit lame but in no pain,
Dan, a scruffy young man, with Shane, a Great Dane,
Walking ahead and sniffing the ground,
On the well-trimmed green grass verges around.

Running up from a short narrow lane,
Suddenly Sam nastily attacks Shane,
Snapping, snarling, maybe a bite,
Shane runs off out of sight.

An elderly gentleman hearing the commotion,
Calls Sam in with great emotion,
Outside the front door of his house,
Kowed he saunters in quiet as mouse.

Bumping into a cyclist they nearly collide,
Whilst running back to Dan's side,
Shane reappears fearful but bright,
With not a bite in sight.

Barking, running wild on the ground,
Joyful Sam is no longer around,
A welcome sight to Dan's delight,
Thankful Shane his pet Great Dane is alright.

M J Harris (Liskeard)

Celebrating A Man Of Words

One hundred years of Betjeman John
One hundred years - where has it gone?
One hundred years of flowers and trains
Pictures in words from seats upon trains.

Over the bridge - the viaduct too
Under a hillside, there was always a view
His visions of people - who came and who went
He had a way with words - this clever gent.

Included in poems were Reading and Slough
He wrote about piggies and also the cows
His poems had purpose - and also - function
Somewhere in his poems was Evercreech Junction.

It is a long while since he passed away
We give thanks for Sir John who came our way
I wonder if ever, we shall again see his like
A man who made poems about a man on a bike

Turning ordinary people into pictures with words
Describing with gusto - the sounds of the birds
He lives on in his poems - about you - about me
He will always be with us,
                        and that's how it must be.

Trevor Vincent (Somerset)

The Somerset Levels

Sodden, soaked, fields to the left and the right
Dank, damp, chill, in the drear winter light
Rain followed rain, water logging the earth
Driven on by gales, to give the floods birth
Still now, like glass, trees reflect on their face
The levels, a truly watery place
Though once it was sea, and could be again
If the polar caps melt, the sea height will gain
No sea wall on earth could keep back that force
Bludgeon and follow its natural course
To the foot of the Tor, round it would lap
Wipe many places right off the map
Godney lighthouse come again to the fore
Moorlynch have fishermen call at their door
Land of the islands once more we would be
Same as when Joseph came from Galilee
In the lap of the gods is our destiny
Be it sun, flood or even the sea.

Dora Watkins (Bridgwater)

Bristol And Brunel '200'

Isambard Kingdom Brunel; Bristol honours him with pride.
He designed our Suspension Bridge, 'cross the Avon Gorge divide.
'Twas finished in 1864 - alas, by then, Brunel had died.

Designed for horse-drawn carriages, he'd have marvelled at the sight
Of petrol-driven motor cars now crossing day and night,
And of Concorde passing overhead as she makes her final flight.

After railways and bridges, Brunel's designs turned to sea,
And the SS Great Britain, the first iron-steamship, launched in 1943.
Now ocean-going passengers could sail the seas in luxury.

She made many trips to Australia, 'til she was scuttled by fire,
But in 1970 was towed home again; rescued from her watery pyre.
Now she resides in Bristol docks; her glory restored for all the admire.

Brunel was born in eighteen o'six, and died aged fifty-three.
Yet his remarkable achievements survive for us to see.
Worth celebrating two hundred years on, I'm sure you will agree.

Gwen Hoskins (Midsomer Norton)

Christmas Village

Our village at Christmas is so cheerful,
all the little coloured lights
twinkle on the tree.
The hall has many people
gathering to buy fruit and gifts
and paper angels
the children have made.
Young and old sing hymns
and carols at the church,
they sing to Jesus and Mary
about the days of old.
It is so cheerful here
and as the daylight fades
most people make their way home
to their cottages along the lanes,
as it lightly snows.
A celebration of Christmas
our village at Christmas
is a joy to behold.

Anita Kavanagh (Exeter)

The Outsider

Imagine . . .
A book with no pages,
A group of children playing together and just one . . . all alone,
A television with no picture,
A group of sunflowers growing together and one . . . all alone,
    Just imagine you being left till last . . . every time.

Imagine . . .
A shoe with no lace,
Children ganging up on you calling you names . . . all the time,
A candle with no flame,
    Just imagine you being left till last . . . all the time.

Imagine . . .
A piece of writing with no punctuation,
A heart with no love,
A lake with no water,
    Are you alone?

Imagine . . .
A pen with no ink,
A bird with no song,
A beach with no sand,
    Just imagine being left all alone . . . being the outsider.

Bethany Priddis (11) (Somerset)

Weston

Meeting at the bus station
I help a stranger with her bags
and then you put a smile on my face
I treat myself to a (sandwich) breakfast
and then we wait
a queue of many
for the journey
to a sandy, sunny day
We arrive
at a promenade café
we then discuss our (activity) options
a pub, the beach, the shops
thus splintering into groups
we head off
and I choose to go to a chip shop
where I am visually distracted
by a perfectly placed bikini
I walk onto the sand
and I eat my chips
and some grains of sand
persuading me to explore the pier
where I discover a hat shop
and within a cheap sun hat
my head I place
cooler now as I paddle
in the waves
my mind wanders
to treasure and trinkets
so I head off towards the market
and there with all my money spent
the best thing this day
is the companions
with which it was spent.

Kevin Pearce (Bristol)

Romany Man

Gypsy man, Romany man -
person I'm proud to know.
Horsemaster and healer,
Seer and dreamer.

Romany speaker;
a language I don't understand
but your lifestyle -
that, I do.

Wandering, roving,
blown before the wind.
A piebald to pull your wagon,
trotters for the fair
and lurchers for the coursing -
all you have
is all you need.

The free air,
a campfire and the sunset;
nowhere called 'home'
except the open road
in the country of your birth.

A lifestyle which vanished long ago,
that most will never see;
Gypsy man - I think you're luckier
than any of us will ever know.

Rose Taylor (Truro)

A While On Dartmoor

When I awoke this morning,
I thanked God for this day
I looked out of my window
And saw the sun at play.

So I walked up to the beautiful moor
And was filled with great elation
I sat high up on the rugged Tor
To gaze at God's creation.

I sat in peaceful solitude
Many colours I could see
For the moor was in her brightest mood
As nature let her be.

The gorse had donned her yellow dress,
The hawthorn pink and white
The heather will soon be at her best
I beheld a wonderful sight.

Sounds in the distance I could hear
The bleating of the sheep
Amidst a bird song - oh so clear!
Spring has wakened from her sleep.

So now I must wander from the moor
Leave its moods and mystery
For Dartmoor's ever open door
Is steeped in glorious history.

Betty Prescott (Tavistock)

Love

Sun-drenched, wind-blown, sea-splashed
Your last earthly place of rest,
As you gaze across the water
To Godrevy, facing west.
Yet the shadow stretching over
Of Montbretia, as it blows
Speaks of far-off country gardens
Where this pretty flower grows.

Childish tears, teenage joys, adult fears,
But always from your birth,
The softly waving, golden corn,
The birdsong and the earth.
And then we came to Cornwall
And your tree of life grew wide,
Happiness and friendship
Marched forward, side by side.

Sun-drenched, wind-blown, sea-splashed,
The laughter filled our days,
Everyone became your friend
With your gentle, winning ways.
The years were filled with loveliness,
A gift so fine and rare,
As I think of your love and joy
I now they're gifts to share.

Hilary Greensmith (St Ives)

Distant Hills Where Rainbows Die

Distant hills where rainbows die
Live still in fading memory
And sleep makes fast with heavy eyes
Those who would recapture.

Brash winds subdued by lovers' tears
Do no more than softly ruffle
And gently wake forgotten dreams
Rainbows everlasting.

A P Dixon (Basingstoke)

The Herring Gull

Operatic elation as their offspring pass
And trumpets of excitement
As they complete their flight tasks.

'Fly, fly, fly,' urging them on
Teaching their juveniles competence and strong.

Then hunger sighs while they monitor the air
And anxious quacks at their weariness there.

Landing to feed with caution not greed
Polite rations with appreciation indeed.

Breathtaking beauty both young and old
Oozing charm and charisma
And majesty untold.

Like flying heralders they dance gracefully on high
The Great Maker's theatre
Exalting the sky.

Then snow-capped mountain knowing brow
From beige-white feathers' softest hue.

Modest nobility elegant and true
And innocent naivety shining through.

Diligent students navigating the skies
And growing in confidence as time goes by.

Tutored at Gull School immaculate throng
Lined up on rooftops doing nothing wrong.

Patiently waiting elders' instruction
And sorties carried out
And disciplined induction.

Born brown fluff
Then brown and white young
Then stunning white down
And great stateliness come.

Liz Taylor (Worthing)

The River

Large boats and small boats all down by the river
Steamers and ferries and sails of all sorts
The liners are coming into Southampton
Then sailing again for far-distant ports

I wish I was sailing to some of those places
With company and sunshine and new things to see
And visits to places quite strange for the travellers
And days just sailing the wide open sea

The days would pass quickly but would I be happy
Thinking of home and the river near me
Of the large boats and small boats and Port of Southampton
This, I think, is the place for me.

Norma Perrin (Southampton)

A Seaside Town

A seaside town
Or a town by the sea?
It does not matter to you or me.
From the arcade the children espy
The sea, 'The sea, I see it,' they cry,
The wonder, the thrill, the endless flow
On their young faces such joy does glow.

Sea salt bites and gulls cry screeching,
Sun shines bright and cuttle fish lie bleaching,
Candyfloss and ice cream drips,
The pungent smell of fish and chips.

Dodgem rides, seaside rock and kites,
Old 'uns, young 'uns and little mites
By the seaside enjoying their day,
'Mum, Dad, please let us stay.'

Tightly clutched buckets and spades,
The skimming of roller blades,
Fishy smells as we draw near,
Boats, nets, lobster pots by the pier.

Crazy golf and amusement machines,
Sleepers in deckchairs - masters of dreams,
A seaside town
Or a town by the sea?
This is the place for me.

Sylvia Olliver

In The Sky

I see the sky
I see the blue
I know my husband is up there too

I see the birds
I see the planes
But I long to have him home again

I see the clouds
I see the sun
I know he is having so much fun

I see his smile
I see his face
I now know he is back home and safe.

Susan Wells (Farnborough)

Nature's Library

Mother Nature surrounds us in all her glory
No author could write such a wondrous story
A Mills and Boon romance
Swans' necks entwined on a shimmering lake
A mystical tale
Of snakes swaying, hypnotically staring
A mystery thriller
Whose footprints break the virgin snow?
A comedy of errors
Of skittish lambs, leaping and bleating
A children's fantasy
Of eagles, of mountains and far-off lands
The story of life evolving
Is ever-growing, ever-revolving
The book unfolds
Leaves ever-turning
New chapters beginning
Nature is an endless story.

J Hedger (St Leonards on Sea)

Titanic

The Titanic, what a beautiful ship,
But what a dreadful thing to happen on that doomed trip.

If only the ship hadn't struck that huge piece of ice on that fated night,
For the people on that ship, there are so many words to describe
how they would of felt, one is sheer fright.

The ship was never supposed to sink to the bottom of the sea,
Until the iceberg struck the people aboard were full of glee.
That dreadful night will never be forgotten, what a sad night,
If only another ship had been around to see the flares go up
into the night sky, they were really bright.

Not enough boats, how sad, how could that be,
More people could have been saved not been taken by the sea.

To imagine being on that ship fills you with dread,
But now her resting place is on the bottom of the seabed.

She rests where she landed all those years ago,
One by one her lights went out, she was no longer aglow.

Karen Grover (Farnborough)

A Part Of Yesterday

Walking in time-faded footsteps that were trod so many years ago.
Through same cobbled lane to recollect youth that brought
happiness and so.
That wall I clambered over is still there although the scrapes
and bruises are all gone.
My make-believe retreat to adventure which childhood dreams
were based upon.
The old house still emits its sense of aura, the dark attics that were
so long my humble abode.
Where brother and sister tales of haunting were created
and spine-tingling hair-raisingly told.
The memory of those endless flight of creaking stairs totalling
thirty-six in all.
I wonder, is my name still there on the landing which I discreetly
etched on the wall.
I dwell to look up at those old unpainted windows, is my imagination
playing those same old tricks on me?
A strange and wonderful feeling sweeps through my mind,
is that my face at that window I see.
One cherishes childhood thoughts and dreams created to entertain
an energetic mind.
It warms my old heart to see part of my yesterday has been
deliberately left behind.
Left behind as proof of being a part of my parents' pride and joy.
To my parents a place they called their palace and me their little boy.
A little boy who has grown into a man who returns
to reflect once more,
Who now wonders what was it now like on the inside, darest
he knock on the door,
That door he had so many times passed through to which
he once held a key.
But sadly a hesitant hand and second thoughts, the knock
on the door was not to be.
So I walk away in comfort to dwell on the future not the past.
To seek fulfilment in my fondest thoughts and make them forever last.

R C Craddock (Havant)

The Way Us Is

Tis bootiful yer in debin,
Some volks say, s us is maze
But they, m always yer on holiday, they stands and watch the cattle
graze,
Walking down the country lanes, they spots the local pub
Us might be maze,
But most of all, they likes ar olsome grub
Zum zinks a pint of zider the village varmer made,
Then they zounds even dafter, as they makes their way to bade,
They zeems to think us stands about, wiv straw between ar teef
Fitted out in long white smocks, wiv nort else underneef,
They likes to visit all the varms, feeding this and that,
And wish they ad ar wellie boots when they find their first cowpat,
There's nowhere quite like debin, us got a lingo of ar own
And if city volks don't like it,
They'd be better off at home.

Marcia Luxon (Exeter)

Down Our Way

Would you like to live here, down our way?
It has for and against, but come what may
It's home to some great folk for work and for play.
There are a few shops, Post Office and pubs,
A Church in the centre, also some clubs.
There's the 'Evergreen' oldies, the WI, a football team;
Then we all sigh at the sight of the rubbish tip, power station bold.
But everyone's welcome into our fold.
I came as a bride forty-seven years since;
To a local young man - and really my prince.
We brought up two daughters and have grandsons four,
I'm sure we will stay here, we have friends galore.
So if you pass by, please stop, then I'll say;
Don't go, you're most welcome to come
Down our way.

Anne Baker (Sutton Courtenay, Abingdon)

That Blessed Hour

It's the hour before the hour that was.
It's the time before the time that was.
We have that straight, then just
as we adjust to taking tea
and cake at three
instead of four,
on the hour that was
before the hour that was,
time passes and the hour that is,
is now beyond the hour that was.

Doreen Fay (Portsmouth)

Constant Bracklesham

The view remains.
A curving segment of stony shore,
From Selsey Bill
To that immovable steel sail
Forever still.

The bay changes.
Gulls claim their yearly re-possession.
With swoops and shrieks
Irascibly they drown the shouts
Of summer weeks.

Real and unreal.
Glass-floored sails which never billow
Anchored not free.
Castles of sand, child-dug canals
Run to the sea.

Actual, virtual,
Tangled together like twisted weed
Washed ashore,
False and true, sorted through, smoothed clean
The tide wins once more.

Pamela Courtney (Bracklesham Bay)

My Pet Spider

When you try everything
And nothing works out
Don't get depressed
Take a leaf out of
My pet spider's book.

He never gives up
He weaves and weaves
If he doesn't catch a fly
He lives on in another guise
His name's Boris and he never lies.

Once he said to me,
'Please don't be down,
Bad times always end,
Just like the good ones never last,
In the end, you'll have the last laugh.'

So I wrote off to a publisher
With his idea and he said,
'I'll take him on -
I've never heard of a spider
With such pluck.'

And I sent him off in an envelope
To Indility, South Hants
He wrote to me saying,
'I love it here - miss you lots,
But I'm afraid I like the flies here
Lots and lots.'

But in the end the flies ran out
And he trotted back to me
Along roads and roundabouts
Until he was outside my door
Without a doubt.

Because he had been away
The flies had fed on the food
While there was a lack of webs
So in he went, started weaving, weaving
Until they all fled.

So him and me, we had a celebration
We popped open a bottle of Burgundy
And we got drunk.
And in the morning
He was a groggy spider - we were mates.

After we'd chatted for a while
He realised he was a tired spider
And I was a tired bloke
So he went to his web
And I went back to bed.

Grant Ruby-Murray (Cuckfield)

The Moon's Children

I am floating like a cloud
But with a vague sense of purpose
Wandering across a field
Fragrant with rain and grass
My intent, though floating as I was
Sharpens as I come across
A smooth white moon shimmering,
Nestling in the grass.
My knife, sharp and satisfying
Slides through the stalk and then, behold!
A mushroom, gills still innocent and pink
Texture; suede, silken, the delicate perfume
Intensifies as I lightly brush away
The errant strands of grass that
Cling desperately to something
More wonderful than they . . .
I heed not their pleas, but with gentle
Hand discard them one and all.
Carefully I place the perfect miniature moon
Away in my cloth bag,
Simple pleasure in my heart.
Back again go I to my wandering search,
Enjoying the sun, the sky, the birds,
The cows as they chew lazily upon nettles -
I cannot help but wince - my supper shall
Be vastly more appetising!
A gift of sun and of rain, a gift from nature
To me (and my satisfied stomach).

Amy Pluess (Eastbourne)

On The Level

They said, 'He's on the level -
Honest, straightforward, someone you can trust -
On the level.'
And down in Somerset I could see him,
On the Levels
From Othery to Chilton Poldon,
Galumphing in galoshes,
Flushing out herons,
Hooting at hares,
Disturbing an indignation of Canada geese;
Or walking broodily over the squashy miles
Of cow-dunged pasture, flat as their pancake.

The rhines in-between were full of supercilious swans.
(They can break a man's arm,
And behave unspeakably to women!
Look at Leda)
Wet winds sweep over the Levels
with only a bending willow
Or black-catkinned alder
To halt their progess to Bridgwater Bay.

The churches are full of ghosts of soldiers
Penned up and murdered in Western Zoyland Church.
Perhaps they have become swans, the aristocrats, that is,
While the compelled peasants are only Canada geese.
That's what's called finding your own level.
The old Abbott was on the Levels too.
He started all that earnest drainage by the honest sweat
Of his workers' brows.
Was he on the level?
It depends where you start.

V M Cornford (Yetminster)

The Place

I once knew a place where the colours were brighter
The blacks were blacker, the whites were whiter,
The horrors more chilling, the pleasures intenser -
There was magic abroad, the horizons immenser.

We all can recall a haunting place
On the edge of perception, not seen face to face,
Which with diligent search slips farther away,
Like the rainbow's end on a changeable day.

I yearn to return there, I long to go back.
How could I forget the route to the track
That leads to such treasures, the promised land,
When I once knew the way like the back of my hand?

That morning glory world of the child
Where love was unstinted and let us run wild,
Is discovered briefly in ravishing dreams,
Through tunnels of nightmares in slight golden seams.

S R Hawk'sbee (Crowborough)

The Place To Live

The place to live is by the sea
Cockles and whelks and afternoon teas
Kiss me quick hats, Rossis ice cream
Soon becoming a passing dream
The dear old pier burnt down three times
Will it ever rise from the ashes?
So much money has been wasted
Yet still not achieved the beautiful landscape
That is but our dream
Our dear old band stage still in store
We want back our music and concerts galore
Beautiful restaurants suit all
Children's activities back on our pier
Band stage restored in appropriate place
Couples dancing and falling in love
The cliffs with the sea views for all to enjoy
Little children playing on the shore
A high street with fountains and flower beds galore
A skating rink and roller ring for all to enjoy
Fat cats in office have spoilt it for us
Throw them out of office and give Southend back

Elsie Moore (Southend-on-Sea)

Seaside

The streets are long, and quite widely,
with lots of houses spread each side.
People coming, people going
others in gardens doing the mowing.
Buses come and buses go, either side of the road you know,
in to town, getting shopping done
then on to beach, children having fun.
Ice cream in hands, the weather hot,
seeing friends, some we thought forgot.
People on holiday looking around
talking of bargains they have found.
Evening comes, time for leisure.
Playing bingo, if it gives you pleasure.
A drink with friends or maybe a show
enjoying themselves wherever they go.
Till time runs out and nights are calling,
back home to bed and eyelids falling,
dreaming of holidays when next comes around,
meeting new friends that you have found.

Jean Smith (Bognor Regis)

Thing?

Thing? What thing d'you think you've lost?

                They search in word spaces.

        What rattled up vacuum tube wasn't just dost.

      What's 'dost', new computer term? That gone missing, too?

           You'll learn. Take machine apart.

Expect you've a cold, have you? Serves you right for a start.

                Been misery since wedding finger tossed

        Stone over knuckle that frosty cold night.

           Warming chuckle.

        What they find he politely replaces,

                 This with a kiss.

K M Lane (Sandown)

The Lifeboat

A young lad staring out to sea,
Was looking very sad,
Tears were running down his face,
As he remembered his dear dad.

His dad, he was a lifeboatman,
Who one day had a call,
To save some people on a craft,
That had got caught in a squall.

The sea that day was very rough,
When the lifeboat pulled out to sea,
His dad had waved, shouted goodbye,
Called, 'I hope we'll be back by tea.'

Teatime came, the lad went down,
To stand there by the shore,
Waiting for the lifeboat's return,
As he had done, many times before.

He waited, and he waited,
Then he heard someone call,
'Come on away home now, lad,
For your dad's boat, will not return at all.'

The lifeboat was dashed against the rocks,
And all hands had been lost,
The men, had gone out to save others,
But their lives had been the cost.

So each year now upon that day,
The lad stares out to sea,
Remembering the day his dad waved goodbye,
But never came home to tea.

Maud Eleanor Hobbs (Basingstoke)

Can It Be?

Ye tossing tide be constantly upsurging on the shore,
Each billow's roll so restless be beyont a little more.
And gradual outspreaded there, for just a while or so -
A blue lagoon, and very soon 'tis where us children go.

We're paddling and wading in wi' fishing nets and sticks,
And poking here, and prodding there at crabs and duckling chicks.
All in among the craggy rocks and caverns steeped with eld -
Where some say Guy de Blackeneye was treacherously felled.

O how the years hath ruined it, since when those idyll days -
Wi' jam jars on a piece of string innocuously we plays.
When all the world was miles away, and all the village ours,
As when old Jake sat on a rake - the rest of us sent flowers.

We were a tight community wi' names of ages long,
The Beardlaws and the Cotebys and the Shellabeers among -
The many on the tombstones here, though one thee can't deny
Stands out a mile, and brings a smile, be Guy de Blackeneye.

He's underneath a wizened yew, and very nicely kept,
'Sir Guy de Blackeneye' it says, 'How all of us hath wept.
Thou's brought prosperity and rum, thy derring-dos were rife,
Until thee got too much buckshot, and forfeited thy life.'

O how the years hath ruined it, since when those florid tones,
The blue lagoon hath been replaced by bistros, lights and cones -
A marina, and a fairground, and multi-national noise,
O can it be, 'tis only me rue rogues and fisher boys.

D Haskett-Jones (Beaminster)

Seven Deeds Of Mercy

(A 14th century mural in Trotton Church, Sussex. Clothing the naked. Feeding the hungry. Visiting the sick. Comforting the prisoner. Giving drink to the thirsty. Lodging the stranger. Burying the dead)

The naked

Shivering poplar-white, sore-crotched, heel raw
poised over stones. Material intercession
cradles his foot. His shrivelled fingers thaw,
clothing the proffered mantle of compassion.

The hungry

A hollow stare. The rivers of his strength
consumed by deserts. Fortune's parody.
An aching cave of emptiness. Its length
diminished by the bread of sympathy.

The sick

Sleep a deception. Pain his chanticleer.
He burrows looming prospects of distress.
Expanding flowers sunrise his cloistered fear
and lavish aromatic tenderness.

The prisoner

Stench. Rusting iron. Youth made middle-age.
The world accommodated in his cell.
A smuggled smile eliminates his rage.
His tumbling walls reveal the merciful.

The thirsty

Skull pounding. Itch of trickling salted sweat.
Clawed prickly heat. A splintered pestilence.
He inundates his body, drowns his throat
ecstatic in a chill benevolence.

The stranger

Stranger! Suspicion. Furtive keys. Lean dogs
ferocious-fanged. Dark rectangles one-eyed.
A kindly voice eliminates his rags
and hoists him over balconies of pride.

The dead

The good man's labour is a lively dance.
He melts the frozen laughter of the dead.
In tombs he spills the seed of renaissance
and sweating comfort he is comforted.

Peter Gillott (Warminster)

Big Brother

Have you ever felt that feeling,
as if someone else is there,
or felt as if someone is following you,
or watching you, but where?

Well, my friend, I must say,
and other people say this too.
That feeling that you get, my friend,
is Big Brother watching you.

Hayley Briant (14) (Southampton)

Sussex Home

A cottage inland. Enough to see the sea
In the distance, past the farmland, down the lane.
I live at last where I have longed to be
In a peaceful part of Sussex helping me regain
The memories of past visits when I was very young.
Swish of waves and freedom to explore the rocks and pools.
Fish to see and fish to eat and happy to be among
The laughter and the love, not minding we were fools
To think it might be lasting longer than a week!
But it can go on forever now I'm older and I'm here.
I've lived and loved and learned a lot, and still to reach my peak.
I'll settle in maturity in the county I hold dear.

Ivy Gallagher (Bexhill-on-Sea)

Where I Live

I live in a place where the sun always shines
And people are happy, not sad
Where love and praise go hand in hand
And nothing's ever bad
Where children sing and play all day
And always sleep at night
Where grass is green and flowers bloom
And everything's just right
Where neighbours smile and help each other
And never ever fight
Where roads are free of traffic
And everything's all right
Where no one sees a doctor
Or ever takes a pill
Because they are all pain-free
And never ever ill
This place of heaven where no one knows
Is not a place to dread
The saddest thing about it is
I live inside my head

Patricia Taylor (Bournemouth)

My Cotswold Collection

Homely abodes of honey-coloured heaven
Nestle amidst the hills I love
Crystal streams to which I'm given
Reflect the sky's glory from above

First to Bourton and its bridges in beauty
Crossing the Windrush waters so clear
To visit you must and honour the duty
'Tis at the heart of this region so dear

Then on to Stow at the height of the hills
So charming, so quaint and so fair
Antique and book shops, its streets they're filled
With a unique and endearing air

Down Fish Hill and into Broadway
In Worcester and not in Gloucs'
Teddy bear shops and cute tea stops
A haven in which to be lost

Along the Fosse and enter The Slaughters
Upper and Lower both rare
Cast an eye over Mill on the water
And while away pure time there

Through mellow sun of winter or summer high shine
The warmth of these Wolds burns through
Weaving their magic with every incline
And every honey cottage in view

K Smette (Banbury)

Shoreham Summer

A shrunken Adur under lazy boats
Too stuck to rock and roll or play mud larks.

We leave them sleeping, go to find the sea . . .
Beyond the pebbled agony of feet
Sand stretches further than we've ever seen
towards the shimmering water far away
Where distant tiny figures disappear,
Distorted ghosts from Lowry's painted scene.

Yet Shoreham's nothing like dark Manchester
In those days smoking with full industry
Where stunted pin-men made the nation's wealth . . .
We're an illusion of low tide, hot sun,
In warm caressing sea we dream away
This magic summer, joying in today.

Con Fraser (Brighton)

The Olden Trails

How simple seemed the pleasures of the park,
How innocent the football with the boys,
Where skies of everlasting blue looked down
And nurtured me among the friends I knew.

Those avenues we wandered after dark
The asphalt beds that ricocheted our noise,
Seem much the same, although the saplings crown
The silver streetlights now they've grown-up too.

On walls and fences fades my boyhood mark,
When we were kings and chalk and other ploys
Were used to designate our patch of town,
But we have come and gone like others too.

I scarcely walk the concrete of the park,
It's more than twenty years since all our boys
Spontaneously converged and ran down
The alleyways to play the game I knew.

Fraser Hicks (Gosport)

Don't Spill The Ink

Show me the child of seven and I will show *you* the adult.
By this age, you can detect the potential for excellence or fault.
Understanding this statement guides us to take heed how we treat
our babies,
Make sure that to our interest and love we give to each of them the
keys.
As they grow, and leave behind nappies, feeding bottles and every
infant lullaby,
Watching them play, their behaviour either causes us shame, or your
head is held high.
When a few years have passed, your soon-to-be-adolescent
starts school,
And through the discipline of learning, the teachers and you discover
if your offspring is angel or ghoul.
If for the wrong reasons your progeny's exploits make the
headline news,
It's only right what everybody says, that it's the adults who raised them
we must accuse.
Remember how fragile these little people are, and need a strong hand
to guide them to a future that's bright.
Children are a blank piece of paper, think carefully before upon them
you write.

Joy R Gunstone (Oxford)

Mirigold Of The Stars

Mirigold was fair,
With beautiful, striking hair,
Of royal blue moon
Flashing and flowing her lips,
Rosy, rosy red lips
She comes in the night,
When she walks
She dashes her cape
In a Merlin-capped face
Creating a path of luck-littered clues
For David,
As she wiles away the magic hours
Mirigold lives
In a glassy white tower,
A world of beauty
Matched only by a flower
Shaping it true, making it blue,
Mirigold was Queen of the British Isles,
In days of old,
When knights were bold,
She blossoms and blooms
A star-studded maze,
A twinkling telescopic haze
Of wondrous praise,
Flashing and blinking the Universe,
A reproducing womb,
To dash-dot wonder
And world of zoom!
Available for you
If just to believe . . . Mirigold,
Destined for you.

David de Pinna (Worthing)

Chase Mill

In the pastoral heart of Hampshire
There's a lucent crystal rill,
There's a half-forgotten mill wheel
By a half-forgotten mill;
And a lawn that stretches westward,
And a peace that reaches deep
Where the bluebells fringe the bracken
And the cronies homeward creep;
And a vision comes before me
In the heat of summer's day
Like a shimmering simulacrum
Of an age long passed away.

There is roistering in the woodland,
In the woods beyond the lane
With many a comely maiden
And many a courtly swain,
And huntsman, hound and hawker
Are gathering in the morn
To the lift of lilting laughter
And the lure of hunting horn,
Till no more am I a dreamer
In this green sequestered place,
But with breathless animation
Riding boldly in the chase.

John M Davis (Eastleigh)

Seating At The County Ground, Hove

At the Cromwell Road end,
The hardy may endure
The slatted wooden seating,
Without an under-layer.

Some sit on folded coats,
Others use inflatables,
Which may be thought as cheating,
Or, worse, not quite respectable.

Those who like to gamble,
Leave fingers in the traps
Of deckchairs demonstrating
A potential to collapse.

And in the old pavilion
One now may watch the game
In plastic tip-up seating
On which is scribed one's name.

These seats replace the benches
Which had to be condemned
For Health and Safety reasons
To the Cromwell Road end.

Michael Irish (Bexhill-on-Sea)

Summer Dusk, Eastbourne

The sky is yellow, orange
and fading into blue.
Suddenly from the north
appears a dark moving cloud
of starlings, weaving into complex
patterns of dark and light,
like fishes from the sea,
fleeing from predators,
faster and faster they go
added to by more starlings
for their final dance
before settling for the night
under the pier.

Elizabeth Jenks (Eastbourne)

Nature

As evening pulls her curtain down and pins it with a star
The nightly sounds of nature are heard from near and far
The scuffling of a badger, the squeaking of a bat
The hooting of an owl, the mewing of a cat
The bark of a vixen calling her mate
The panic of their prey, fleeing from their fate
The hedgehogs stir and dig in the ground
Looking for grubs which from nature abound
The crow of the cockerel, heralding the dawn
The baa of a lamb just newly born
A rustling sound way up in the trees
As the wind gently blows through their elfin green leaves
From a nearby pond, the croaking of a frog
As its courting begins on a half-sunken log
The primroses bloom in the hedgerows in spring
From the tops of the trees the blackbird still sings
A carpet of bluebells covers the glade
And tiny sweet violets hide in the shade
A lovely wild orchid shaped like a bee
There in its beauty for us all to see
All these wondrous things are ours completely free
Nature makes no charges, they're there for all to see
So let's commune with nature, preserve and don't destroy
God's greatest gift to everyone for us all to enjoy.

Peter Lovett (Swanage)

Missing You

The springtime will bring flowers,
to brighten every room.
Alas it will still remind me,
of you and your perfume.

The summer sun and the sea
with footprints in the sand
Will only make me happy,
if I could hold your hand.

The autumn days will get colder
when leaves are changing hue.
But they would not seem so long,
if I could be with you.

Wintertime may bring snow,
with festive Christmas tree.
But I would need no presents
if it was just you and me.

The seasons will come and go,
but nowhere will I find
A lady so sweet and loving,
you are always on my mind.

Jim E Dolbear (Totton)

One Day

I'll write a poem, I said to myself
One day - just for you.
I'll put down on paper the way I feel
About things I hold to be true.

So out came pen and paper too,
Preparing myself for the start,
I marshalled my thoughts, all good and true
And words straight from the heart.

I stared at the paper, so blank and bare
Thinking there must be an easier way,
For the thoughts that I thought were waiting there
Didn't come my way that day.

One day I know I'll write that poem
For all the world to see,
It won't be easy but it can be done,
I'll try hard, real hard - you'll see.

H E Hayward (Worthing)

Coming Home

We've come home
Come back to stay
Never to wander
Far away.
No more sea
No more sand
Just lots of houses
And green grassland.
With friendly faces
Old and new
Familiar places
And lots to do.
So we've come home
This is where we'll stay
'Til I get the urge
To move away.

Linda Francis (Witney)

The Robin

Winter came bringing cold and windy days,
Where sun and moon were scarce upon to gaze,
And yet, a perky robin brought us cheer throughout,
A visitor most welcome, of that there is no doubt.

He proudly showed his breast of red,
Standing bold against the dark and dead.
We hoped and prayed that he would stay,
And so we fed him every day.
And come he did, to give much pleasure,
Then spring arrived to bring its treasures.

One fine day he brought a lady fair,
Indeed they made a handsome pair.
A nest to build was their next chore,
They chose to build by our back door.
Within the hose reel twisted round,
They filled and spun with grass they'd found.

Five blue eggs were laid within,
To wait until new life begins.
Mother watches for shells to crack,
Five orange beaks, feathers fluffy and black,
Emerge at last into the light,
Ten piercing eyes see their first sight.

Gary Murphy (Lymington)

My First Summer With You

Under parcel shade;
each leaf
making up the gentle canopy
of the tree.
Listening to the Summer
to the pure laughter
of happiness.
And as the afternoon sun
beats down
upon the would be boatmen
of the Serpentine
I think of you,
the one that freed me
from my sadness.
Showing the strength
within your tenderness,
my eternal friend.

M Wilson (Bexhill-on-Sea)

Sussex Summer - 2006

Here in the Weald there is no rain;
Deer thrust soft mouths through sharp, silvered grass
Searching for small green shoots
Secreted in the depths.
Butterflies are scattered
Revelling in dry heat:
Stray pheasants dig into bracken
Safe in a sun-proof canopy.
Nettles have grown tall.
This south-east corner
Imitates the pampas.
In this arid year
Summer is a different colour.
Blossom time soon passed;
Apricot roses lost definition
As cacti expanded under glass
Shooting out cerise and yellow flowers,
Usurping space once held by
Thirsty fruit and dahlias.
A slatted seat bears witness
To cracks in earth below.
Horse-chestnut trees
With rust-shrivelled leaves
Bend low with blight.
Pigeons sink clumsily
Into man-made pools of water;
Nesting time soon over
One brood was quite sufficient.
Here in the shadow of the Downs
There is no rain.

Veronica Charlwood Ross (Cuckfield)

This Life, This Earth, This Cosmos

The eating
The drinking
The laughter
The sleeping

The look
The talk
The appointment
The meeting

The whole
The part
The soul
The heart

The vision
The idea
The preparation
The start

The birth
The growing
The education
The knowing

The seed
The root
The plough
The sowing

The beauty
The passion
The love
The compassion

The eye
The drawing
The creation
The fashion

The earth
The space
The smile
The face

The turmoil
The anguish
The language
This place

Dave Arnold (Hastings)

Cave Of Lost Dreams

Across the blackened sea upon a boat of timeless dreams,
There I sit in the smoked moonlight,
A haze of painted blurs.
Waters flowing with diamond dots as we hear this cavern's tale.
The Rustic three begin to chime,
Chaotic murmurs, bewitching notes,
Nymphs and mermaids peer between.
Florescent silk coral sways light below,
The murk beneath lays dead and slow.
Porous holes within the walls breathe life to chills and cold.
And in those pillars lapsed waters rise,
And mark our errors and our ways.
Two symbols put out from us within
To test our hopes, to tarnish our dreams.
Now that you're here, there's no looking down,
Stay close to the surface, underneath you is tar,
Eels of fear and titans of the mind,
Will prey on you and curse your sight.
Inside a silver painted box,
A symbol of destiny points sharp,
A sword of hero's untimely defeat,
And the darkest painting of a creature on card.
The beast and sword lay in my hands,
As the silence deafeningly fell.
The beauties peered, eyes talking to me,
Those diamond dots dimmed,
And shunned out the sea.
The moonlight dropped and fell from the sky,
And then I understood the wheres and the whys.
The journey I took as I drifted from above
Into a cave where I freely could believe,
And learn the test of creating my dreams.
Each bubbling dream,
Every magical idea,
Is paired with a beast who will try to ensnare.

But in that box, a weapon of defeat will
Curse that demon and allow you to be free.
Across the blackened sea I went,
In search of my lost dreams,
I found them waiting in my place,
Where heroes rule the ragged seas.

Anna Green (Yapton)

Clouds Of Butterflies

I lived a lifetime one summer
With your smile to light my day
Of golden hours, and balmy nights
And clouds of butterflies
The grass was never greener
Sky so blue it looked unreal
Rainbows without rain shone bright
Over clouds of butterflies
The autumn came, time to part
Away you went to achieve your fate
Left behind 'midst falling leaves
No clouds of butterflies
I would not have missed one second
Of our life beneath the sun
Next year for others may there be
Clouds of butterflies.

Jackie Painter (Brighton)

Reflection

Reflection to me is meditation and musing
It is a slow process of pondering and thought
Likewise it is a deliberation of ideas,
Giving the ideas consideration,
Which takes much longer as the years go by?
The photo album is a stimulus,
Reflecting over past events
I sit and meditate and observe
But are those impressions as I remember them?
Do I review them in a different way
Has my opinion of the impression changed with age?
Yes, it throws a different light on the vent of this I am sure

Patricia Allen (Ventnor)

The Beauty Of Dorset

The giant stands on hills at Cerne,
His origin folks try to discern;
At Sherborne, castle stands supreme,
For countless folk it is a dream.

At Portland Heights the views are great,
The Chesil Beach it is first rate;
The Pulpit Rock at tip of Bill,
Gives stories for our mind to fill.

Gold Hill at Shaftesbury oft in news,
Surrounding country gives great views;
The woods and lanes create great joy,
Bring pleasure to adults, girls and boys.

The Dorset coast is truly great,
The view and scenes make first-class date;
The tanks at Bovington are bettered by none,
At Morden lies Lawrence, with his work long done.

The Stour at Blandford winds its way to the sea,
The Georgian town just as good as can be;
The harbour, at Poole, so busy with freight,
Brownsea Island so peaceful, a romantic date.

The Great Dorset Steam Fair takes place every year,
The engines a picture, and the horses bring tears;
This county of Dorset, with its streams and its dales
Offers beauty, splendour and great Hardy tales.

John Paulley (Blandford Forum)

Message From Connie

Have you ever,
In some disconnected scene,
Suddenly been transported
To a moment of the past?
When some indefinable signal,
Like a half-seen flash of light
On a black horizon,
Awakens the very sight
And sound and smell
Of that time of long ago.
And for one heart-gripping moment
All around vanishes
And you are hurled
Back in time and place?
Such it was then,
As I sat enveloped in the music
That throbbed and beat around me.
And try as I might
I could only reach and touch
The soft hem of the memory,
And was filled
With an infinite sadness.
Nobody has told me,
But I know she is gone.

Paul Motte-Harrison (Shoreham-by-Sea)

The Quiet Bay

I close my eyes but always see
that stretch of golden sand
with cliffs of ebon rock which
seemed to tempt a rolling sea.

And far off with discerning eye
small boats were tossed upon
the daring waves professing
calm but smashed their way

Along the coast causing some
anxiety but calm restored
with human faith recharged
the bay began to smile again

With craggy rocks that dried
their salty tears and azure
sky smiled blue and sea was
calm, I thought I'd dreamt

It all, but no it was not so,
for I am here on holiday
in my favourite bay with
serenity called Cornwall.

Ann Safe (Hastings)

Ode (Owed) To Amberstone

I had a painful wrist in '83;
The doc advised me to go for therapy;
So, feeling nervous and shy,
I walked to Hellingly;
With care and hot wax, it was 'Bad wrist, bye-bye.'

And then the nagging aches of age were mine;
Arthritis in my knees and hips and spine;
The doc replied to my moan,
'Go to Amberstone,'
And now my knees are feeling fine.

'Lie on something hard and *STRETCH* and rest;
Point your toes to north, south, east and west,
Roll right and then left, don't moan . . .'
Since going to Amberstone,
Spine, hips and knees are nearly at their best.

And now my shoulder (right) is under par.
Kind John and Barry take me in by car
Each week to Amberstone
For heat and pulley and so on,
And exercise at home . . . it's better by far.

For physio, three cheers - hip hip hurrah!
Hands, knees and boomps-a-daisy - Ha ha!
Since visiting Amberstone
Most of the pains have gone!
It's so much better than wishing on a star!

Dorothy M Parker (Hailsham)

A Sonnet To The Selfish

Each dawn they shatter our rural idyll;
Those dog-owning townies in four-by-fours
Who wake us from dreams, we could enjoy still,
If it wasn't for their slamming of doors,
After letting out Duke, Rover or Spot,
To whimper and snarl, to yelp and to bark.
They're mean and selfish; concerned not a jot,
For us who don't wish to rise with the lark.
They scream and shout 'fetch' or 'leave and come here',
To their poorly trained or cretinous muts,
Then abuse their cronies when they appear;
'You've got no control'; 'Are you effing nuts?'
It's time these townies faced some restrictions,
To save sleepy souls from such afflictions.

Edward Lyon (Sandown)

Oxon's Leafy Lanes

Driving through the countryside
Month later it's a by-pass
Leaves are disappearing
Disappearing so damn fast
If not for automobiles
Some gone by estates
Even the local pub
It is wine bar now, mates
So Oxon's leafy lanes
Not cow or horse with drover.

Michael D Bedford (Oxford)

Reflection Upon 'Potential'

A flower bud
resembling a tiny clenched fist
against the vagaries of existence
gently begins to unfurl,

petal by petal
until all are open to the world
revealing a beauty
that draws from us
a breath of wonderment.

Then gently
petal by petal has to fall
to reveal something more wondrous
than all that has gone before.

Its seed head,
its heart,
its core.

Within whose outer covering
so intricately designed
lies deep and hidden
a mysterious mechanism
with the potential to become
something different
from its appearance now.

Judith Garrett (Cuckfield)

City Bus Tour

'All aboard . . .' the big open top bus
Waiting patiently for its specky tourists
In Sauchiehall Street . . .
There were plenty of them . . . all brightly painted
With little flags on the side
It was blowing a gale . . . but my aunt didn't seem to mind
She was built for this weather.
I picked up the headphones . . . someone blethering on in Danish
I soon gave up and strained to hear the courier
In broad Glaswegian we took in the sights,
Or rather they took us in , we were a sight . . .
And one for sore eyes at that
A bus-load of tourists out on a culture kick . . . one of these things
. . . As you *DO* . . .
And the bus stopped and started . . . in fits and starts
Noisy children, boring old farts, . . . the famous library
The Museum of Arts . . . the *'HIGHLAND MAN'S UMBRELLA'*
It was only a bridge . . . they say a Scotsman's too mean
And would rather shelter under a bridge than buy a brolly, golly
                                        what a Scrooge
We ate ham sangwidge . . . getting bored I started to fidget
With the clip on windswept hair . . . and Auntie had brought
Some Everton mints, well it was better than nothing
St Andrews towered high above, like a huge wedding cake
She said, 'We'll go there another day . . . ' and I had to be content
                                        with that

We got off the bus . . . two ice cubes later
An old man with a grey beard sat in a shop doorway
Holding out a cap for money . . . he had no teeth, little hair and
                                        bare feet
He must be frozen, and I thought to myself, here was the real sight
To see . . . but people chose *NOT TO LOOK* . . .

Sally Wyatt (North Stoke)

Beautiful Britain

You can go to England, Ireland, Scotland or Wales,
Climbing the hills, or walking the dales.
The weather may not be all we would like,
But it's never so bad you can't go for a hike.
Imagine the Cotswolds when Autumn comes round,
The leaves changing colour, from green, red and brown.
If you live in the south, there's so much to explore,
The Downs, the New Forest and castles galore.
Picturing Wales brings such beauty to mind,
Snowdonia, Swallow Falls, all unchanged by time.
The moors of the north are fine places to walk,
And culture a'plenty in the city of York.
The Angel of the North, so strong and so fine,
Will see you safe over the River of Tyne.
You may try and find Nessie in Scotland's vast loch,
But admire the beauty of Dunbarton's rock.
To know the beauty of Ireland you just have to be
Where the mountains and hills sweep down to the sea.
Wherever you go, north, south, east or west,
This island of ours is the greatest and best.

Vera Brown (Worthing)

Autumn In Future

Time to move away now afresh
Into life's quiet backwater
Leave behind a vast city crush
These mellowing steps will not falter

I have done with the fast race
Cut and thrust office. Step next
into work in a more gentle polite pace
of village life to live by a river, green betwixt

Mornings my joints ache, are less sprightly
In the soft autumn of life's pathway
Maybe the body is not so springy
But still I welcome each happy sunny day

Strolling one Sunday around the village lanes
Between houses spot a tiny farm tucked away
In the orchard are two dapple grey ponies
Quietly feeding on a pile of fresh hay

A dog barks in the distance noisily
The sharp sound not muffled by city rush
Two squirrels chase each other round a tree
Flies zoom, red robin hops in and out of a bush

Along slow meandering footpaths tread
People following a much calmer way
To the quiet place I go and behold
An easier of times and a bright new day

Sheila Cheesman (Southampton)

Sussex

Old Sussex is the place for me
It's still quite green and by the sea.
Although it's not my place of birth
It's the best I've found for goodly worth.
The natives may be broad and solid,
But seldom are recluse or horrid.

New Sussex has seen changes others lacked.
The trains were first before tarmac
made grooved and soggy Wealden clay
into toll-roads then motorway.
The Regent riding down to Brighton
Changed longer route to a short one.
There was less Chapel than further places,
but Norman ones and wild horse races.

Our Hammer ponds look natural now,
but helped the cannon-makers past.
The mighty oaks which clothed the Weald
Were cut down then - their fate was sealed.
These made men-of-war to fight the foe
Our King and country saw them go.

Remember this o'er traffic roar
This is not peace, but that was war.

J W Young (Steyning)

A Winter's Veil

'When will the day begin?'
The veiling of this winter grim
That never seems to lift your chin.
Perhaps a churlish glimpse of light
And then again it is the night.

No sun or moon or stars above
To embrace the Earth with love.
Only wind that whips the floor
And creeks and bends the inner door.

Inside the house snug from the mire
The old dog lays dozing by the fire,
The cat in contemplation sits
Rousing her form to lick her mitts.

As the darkest day expires
To our slumbers we retire.
Tomorrow is another day
And Mother Nature will have her say.

Sheila Lewis (Eastbourne)

To A Wonderful Wife

It's seven long years since I lost you
And it seems like twice those years
Seven years since I last held you
In my arms, amid the tears

Fifty-six years together
To each other always true
You were ever there to help me
When I was down you pulled me through

Nothing is the same without you
Tho' everyone tries to be so kind
But Nell, how can they begin to know
The agony that's in my mind?

In the black and lonely night-time
I turn to stroke your hair
My heart feels empty, broken - lifeless
When I realise you're not there
One day please God I'll join you, up in Heaven above
And we will spend eternity with our undying love

David Merrifield (Winchelsea)

The Seed Of Life

I lifted you from your mother's womb,
The birth of a seed awaiting new life.
Into a pot of love I placed you, alone,
Surrounded by darkness.
In silence you lay, while I nurtured and cared for you.
I gave you warmth, I gave you light.
Waiting, watching, hoping.
So young and fragile you nervously appeared,
Your new beginning, your wanting for life.
You gave me your strength and beauty,
I gave you so little, a chance for life.
Now time has passed with a whisper of sadness
And snatched you from your cherished bed.

Jane Knapton (Ringwood)

The Changing Face Of Ryde

Solitary sands and turbulent seas
A nip in the air and a cool, bracing breeze.
Fluffy white clouds in a bluebell-blue sky,
But Ryde is deserted when winter is nigh.

Ferries arriving all bound for the shore.
Mothers and fathers with children galore.
Sands packed with people who watch for the tide.
Summer is here and the crowds flock to Ryde.

Frances Heckler (Ryde)

Winter

Gone are the swirling, wheeling swifts
Screaming from their playground in
The summer sky.
No more the nightingale sings its litany
In the evening twilight.
Swallows have left their dusty barns,
Martins their mud-formed homes
Under cottage eaves.
Starlings huddle in the darkling trees;
Flycatchers leave the woodland glades
And charms of goldfinches hurry south.

Now the hard, bright winter sun
Lights sparkling dusts of frost on fields and towns.
Chirpy robin preens his scarlet breast,
And skeins of geese from colder climes
Invade our wintry skies,
Honking and whiffling* down to Earth.

Frosted diamonds edge the
Brittle leaves of autumn;
Freezing fog lifts to reveal
Hedgerows thick with old man's beard.
A knife-sharp wind scattered thickening
Snowflakes in eddies and flurries
To powder bare-branched trees,
And hurls sleet, splatting and splintering
On windowpanes.

Windless
Under a brilliant moon
Curls of smoke drift from
Cottage chimneys and
A magic land, covered in its
Shining mantle of still, silent snow,
Meets a silvered sea.

*whiffling - a sound created when geese break formation and swoop
down to earth; the sound could be associated with air whistling
through their feathers.*

K Merle Chacksfield (Isle of Purbeck)

Swanbourne Lake

'Tis gossamer thin, this thread 'tween life and death.
The living breath, the dying breath, 'tis the same breath.
Whether in squeaking swallow summer
Or by the silent ice-swollen lake,
I stand here . . .
People die, change or move away
But there'll always be moorhens,
Their babies with feet like paddle steamers.
There'll be wreckage from old storms
Slithering and sliding into water reflecting
Sycamores and beeches and you'll ask
Which is air and which is water.
And vistas of uplands of sun
Will open like angels' wings.
And sheep, the music of the Downs,
And piles of logs bleaching
For winter fires where we'll warm
With memories of Canada geese like Red Arrows.
And the sound of the train across the plain,
And the blue and yellow boats strung
Like a necklace across the green lake,
And the yellow flag - yellow is for friendship you know -
And we'll come out of the dark valley of trees
Onto the springy downland turf.
And as the sun falls upon the other side,
You'll see the bank of trees rise to the clouds
And your spirit will soar to the blue,
And I'll be very near.
And the heron of the rapier beak;
Probing, preying periscope neck
Piercing the mud for tasty morsels;
He'll glide kite-like and land
Wings spread and ruffled like a lampshade.
The wren will bob and chuckle from stalk to stalk,
And as twilight closes round the island
A mallard cackles and a swan
Shepherds the cygnet to her side.
And the ash tree with its bunch of keys
Waiting to unlock the fruits of autumn.

And all this will be here for you and me
For we are part of nature's plan,
And must listen to the promptings of her inner voice
For we are woven into her sense of time.

Joan Woolley (Arundel)

Gust Of Wind

First a gentle rustle in the leaves,
A sigh, a deep breath from Heaven heaves,
A rush, a scattering, a pattering -
A roar through tortured branches crackling
Dustbin lids like flying saucers wing,
A whistling and whining down the chimneys sing.
Nature's brass and woodwind at the last,
And all the timpany let loose upon the final blast!

Pauline Frost (Rustington)

Bampton Fair

In August the fair comes to Bampton Streets
Roundabouts, bumper cars, candyfloss, sweets,
Hot dogs with onions, beefburgers too,
Chips, humbugs, coconut ice,
All made to tempt you.
But it's not like the old days
When horses were sold;
Gypsies buying and selling with sovereigns of gold.
No cheque book or bank cards were used in those days,
It was cash in the hand, that's how they paid.
Now there's only the rides, the side-shows and stalls,
The one-armed bandits, and rolling the balls.
You might win a coconut, or a fish in a bag,
But for the money you spend you know you've been had.
The prizes are trashy and not worth a cent
But despite everything, you feel glad that you went.
The fair stays three days, and late the third night
All is packed up to move off at daylight.
Streets must be swept, all litter be cleared.
Goodbye Bampton Fair, see you next year!

V C Elward (Oxford)

Cuckmere Haven

Where is my home?
Can I find it here
        where you have never been;
where the coastline breasts the sea
and the whites of the blue eyes
        of the waves
flash smiles of brilliant sunshine
        twinkling merrily?

Where is my home?
Can I find it here
        In this Haven of a dream;
where the cliffs embrace the skies
and the roseate horizons
        of the setting sun
flood many evenings with beauty
        as daylight dies?

Where is my home?
Can I find it here
        where mist obscures the scene
where twilight dew of darkness
and hidden tears of longing
        deep in my heart
mingle with shades of memory
        recalling happiness?

Surely I have found my home.
Surely it is here
        near to where you have been
where moon and starlight shine for me
and the tall white cliffs
        and the white sea foam
speak for ever of your love
        in all its purity.

Rosemary Watts (Seaford)

Love And Kisses: A Rondeau

Sealed with a kiss, the letter that I sent
urging the promise of my heart's intent;
purple with verbal treasures from love's hoard
crafted as offerings to my adored
with skill unusual, by passion lent -

and yet, before the task is done, it's spent:
however much is said, it's half what's meant;
yet I must send it, fervent and yet flawed,
sealed with a kiss . . .

Answer my longings! I shall rest content.
Fulfil my hopes! But know: in the event
of failure to respond to love outpoured
the consequence: betrayal of his Lord
was sealed by Judas - note the precedent -
sealed with a kiss . . .

Sheila Walker (Ottery St Mary)

Loved Inheritance

Oh! *The byways of England* are precious to me,
Of all the Earth's places none dearer could be . . .

Each lane has a beauty, and 'feel' of its own,
    Whatever the season - its mood, or its tone;
The hedegrows hold secrets, and strive to conceal them,
    Yet to sensitive trav'llers they warmly reveal them.
(Is it foolish, I wonder, to muse - passing by -
    If they grow the more proudly, or happily sigh
To thus be an obvious, soul-filled delight,
    And be loved for their changing, yet familiar sight . . . ?)
Behind them, beside them - or within 'rounded' line -
    Sit quaint little cottages. *Oh,* would one were mine!
They nestle so 'comfy' in soil they have known
    For many a year, - so long, they have grown
To be part of the natural scenery there;
    Without them our country would be far less fair!

Apart from the 'quaint' and beautif'lly old,
    Stand the houses of elegance - a joy to behold
Their ample magnificence. So tasteful, serene -
    They offer contentment for hearts there to glean . . .
'Eyes' open and smiling, 'neath 'eyebrows' of thatch
    Look down upon flowers, not minding the patch
Of wayward, yet colourful weeds here and there;
    (Which have nosed their way in for a bit of a dare!)
These dwellings uplift us whene'er we pass by -
    They sweeten our hearts' song, make bright our souls' 'eye' . . .
Such country abodes, be they 'humble' or 'fine'
    Bestow as we view them, a blessing benign.

The anticipation of rustic delight,
    Is so gently enhanced by the beauty bedight . . .
Life's troubles, anxieties, 'lift' from our care
    Just to 'feel one' with Nature - to stand still and stare -
Into trees' canopies, so freshly-green . . .
    So thankful of heart for the wonder here seen . .
. . . The flowers - and grasses - a thicket with nest -
    Each glimpse of delight shared at nature's behest.

Walking on - silently - dear sight to 'enfold' -
    Our approach to a wood! More treasured than gold . . .
What sweet expectation, as, climbing the stile,
    A worn winding path offers peace - with a smile!
To wander its length is so wholly 'renewing' -
    Whilst listening for each tiny sound there; and viewing
The different barks, and leaves of the trees -
    How welcome the delicate sigh of a breeze . .

A stream, so nearby, seems to 'chuckle' along
    Over cobblestones - twisting and turning anon . . .
With great inner longing (not lost - as past youth)
    Our 'wellied' feet plunge in its coolness. Forsooth!
So refreshing to paddle upstream for a while,
    As it gurgles aong with sure haste - even guile!
For suddenly we're almost knee-high in a pool,
    Round a corner - a haven of stillness - so cool . .
The wood holds such joys! (In our hearts ever green.)
    No flower or nook is too humble, to glean
From its very existence, a comforting balm -
    As with each mossy patch . . . a 'carpet' of calm.

To wander the countryside - 'fell' - cliff- or lea . . .
    Is a privilege surely! I feel it to be -
May the 'corners of England' - held deep in my heart -
    Continue to bless, and of life be a part . . .
To soothe, and to nurture the same response ever!
    Alter - deteriorate - disappear? *Never!*

Edna M Stevens (St Leonards-on-sea)

The Day That I Retired And Now

It was a bittersweet experience,
That final day for me.
To say goodbye to many friends,
I'll miss their company.

My brain was really buzzing,
With the plans I had in mind.
Exotic baking, gardening too,
Growing herbs of every kind.

I'll do exercises daily,
Go swimming once a week,
Take our dog the extra mile,
Walking Mengham Creek.

I'll sort photos into albums,
And label every one.
Finish off the sewing jobs,
I have only just begun.

The first year I achieve my aims
Except the swimming bit.
My recipes with home-grown herbs,
Were not always such a hit.

We decided to buy a caravan,
No need to travel far.
To feel the peace - the solitude,
How fortunate we are.

The New Forest on our doorstep,
Watch ponies with their foals,
Walk miles on heathered heathland,
Hear distant bells knoll.

Awake amid the lush green grass,
Inquisitive cows nearby,
Or watch the farmer baling hay,
Evening sun low in the sky.

So many different memories,
Of sight and smell and sound.
Yet we have only just begun,
In the freedom we have found.

God willing we'll have many years,
So much to do and see.
I can recommend retirement,
I'm so happy to be me.

Barbara Servis (Hayling Island)

Ecclesbourne In Summer

So picturesque the yellow gorse-clad clifftop
On a summer's day,
Where linnets sing their melody
And countless rabbits play.

A place of real beauty
Yet so much like a dream,
With a cascading waterfall
From the winding stream.

Spilling down on to the beach below
Of shingle rocks and sand,
And waves rolling in and out
As they reach to caress the land.

The squawking gulls fly out
Across the sleepy bay,
Off into the distance
And far, far away.

In pursuit of the fishing boats
Far out at sea,
While a fulmar glides overhead
A scene of tranquillity.

Looking from the cliffs of Ecclesbourne in summer
A truly breathtaking view,
With glistening rays of sunshine
On the sea so blue.

G Butchers (Hastings)

After The Age Of Seventy-Five

I sometimes check if I'm alive
    It seems to me I'm not here
When I get ignored, I fear.
    Today when paying at the till
The lady there must have been ill,
    A glazed look was in her eye.
As she conversed with a sigh,
    It was the same, to be fair,
That I was not even there.
    I often lay down the law.
My opinions being rather poor,
    But there seems no debate.
No one has heard, it was too late.
    Perhaps I don't speak loud enough
Or my voice has got too gruff.
    The point that I seek to make,
Lost iwth the time I take.
    To the council clerk I seek advice
Having to repeat myself twice.
    She doesn't undertand at all
The point I've made is too small.
    To assert myself I must contrive,
After the age of seventy-five.

G H W (Church Crookham)

My Hometown

I know just the place for a holiday
A place we can all enjoy
It is right on our doorstep, believe it or not
Be we lady or man, girl or boy.

If it's the beach that you like we have miles and miles
Of beautiful, golden sands
We build castles and moats with buckets and spades
And couples walk hand in hand.

The sea is so blue and usually warm
With no pebbles to hurt your feet
An awarded blue flag is hoisted with pride
Under which lifeguards and beach wardens meet.

A National Trust island is great to visit
With plenty of wildlife to see
You reach it by ferry - it's a good day out
And all for a very small fee.

The New Forst is also close at hand
Where ponies and cattle roam
There are many walks with fields and streams
Giving lots of memories to take home.

The Purbeck Hills are not far away
If it's walking or hiking you like
With rucksacks and boots you can walk for miles
And enjoy many breathtaking sights.

So now you know - the secret's out
This hometown of mine by the sea
Is a beautiful place so do come and visit
I'm from Poole in Dorset you see!

Trudi A Hallowes (Poole)

St Mary's, Launceston

As the sun shuts its eyes and sinks westward
shadows hop and jig a fandango on
silent tombstone rows; testimonials
to generations of long lost people.
Here spirits ignore the conformity
of dank graves and enter the church to join
their living cousins at the alter rail.
Saints, dusty from centuries of worship,
peer down from stencilled stain glass windows and
watch as an infant is signed with a cross.
Outside the church, perched high on the wall,
Mary Magdalene's fixed lips become
a stony smile as a rosy red-cheeked
choirboy rushes underneath her archway
and drops a penny by her well for luck.

Heather Nelson (Launceston)

Portrait Of The Sussex Downs

I walk along these tracks, that many have trod before
My beautiful, beautiful Sussex I truly do adore
I am on my own but not alone, how can I be?
Life and nature is at its best, surrounding me.

I come here for some quiet after a busy day
And listen patiently to hear what nature has to say
Sheep are grazing in the fields so peacefully
Looking my way as if to comfort me.

Gladys C'Ailceta (Burgess Hill)

Favourite Places In Carshalton

Old Honeywood House in Carshalton's my favourite place to be
It's full of interesting things
And wandering around it brings
A feeling of how it was in this place
When life was lived at a gentler pace
A fascinating glimpse into the borough's history

It overlooks Carshalton ponds where River Wandle flows
And here you can sit, taking your ease
In the room where they serve teas
Watching ducks and swans as they glide
Babies flapping along beside
While journeying ever onward the little river goes

Then stroll along beside it on a path called Festival Walk
For it's here that you will see
A simply amazing tree!
Quite the tallest in the land
So I'm given to understand
A two hundred-year-old plane! Wonder what it would say if
it could talk?

So it's over North Street Causeway now, thru a doorway in a wall
And here we are inside The Grove
It's such a lovely place to rove
And not very far from here
The lower pond will soon appear
Shimm'ring like a silver ribbon, while skyward wild geese call

While outwards 'neath an old stone bridge, under weeping willow trees
By water wheel and rushes tall
Wandle goes a-tumbling down a waterfall
On along its watery way it weaves
As the beautiful Grove it leaves
Singing a burbling little song full of happy memories

Daphne Lodge (Carshalton)

My Dad

My dad worked hard all his working life
He had a good sense of humour and a gift to tell short stories
When young he played practical jokes on some friends
He loved shooting, walking, golf and bird watching
And encouraged his children in these sports
He loved his spaniels and other dogs
He kept throughout his married life
He wrote a book about his work
He loved Switzerland and other beautiful and old places
Where he and my mother led groups of people on holiday
For 50 years in wartime the holidays were in England
He loved and served God leading Crusader classes
He was a leader in the Anglican church and a ley preacher in
the Methodist
He took services and preached in churches and chapels
Looked after God, took him to his eternal home
Now reunited with my mother
I thank the Lord for my father and his love for his family

Jean Martin-Doyle (St Albans)

The Road To Dulverton

The road winds like a silver thread
Through the valley, and overhead
The clouds with white sails billowing
Move steadily across the sky.
Fallen leaves, bright and glowing still
From yesterday's rain and gales lie
Piled in drifts. On a distant hill
The farmer, a matchstick figure,
Stands motionless while his sheep flow
Through the gate with the fluency
Of molten lava. His collies,
Three black dots, patiently keep low
As they wait for the signal to start,
And then as one they turn and dart,
And swiftly gather in the flock,
Then guide them on the downhill run.

Rosina Winiarski (Dulverton)

Ghost On Highway 41

A silver shadow, ethereal, passing by,
Briefly there, then gone like a dream.
Did you see it?
The sound of tearing metal, screeching brakes,
A human scream hangs in the air
Like the last chords of a mournful violin.

Oh God! An accident ahead,
But further on nothing.
No twisted wreck or broken, bleeding bodies.
Just silence, the dusky light of dawn
And mist drifting across empty fields.

How soon will this beautiful fragile soul, this wraith
Who must cruise the highway of broken dreams,
In the ghost of his beloved car,
Find peace and rest?
Our prayers go with you.
We love you James Dean.

Sheila Giles (Abingdon)

Meg

(1995-2002)

A love is not confined to certain rules;
In many ways we were so far apart.
But what matter if we played and carried on like fools?
The matter was our closeness, not our art.

Who says that two so far cannot be near
In thought, in words unspoken and in love?
What need for separation in our hearts to fear?
We had no need of motives, none to prove.

If people doubt my feelings can be thus
For one so young who could not speak a word,
Let them have witnessed just one hour with us;
Then let them try to label us absurd.

How proud I am to know that you were mine,
My angel, Meg, my beautiful canine.

Maria Lawrence (Totnes)

Black Gold

There is a land so beautiful
that it hurts the eye, sears the soul,
where pastures greened by tumbling rills
creep upwards, sheep-grazed, to the slopes
of daunting heights, cloud-clothed,
mysterious, awesome, grey from their great age.
Silent now, except for sighing winds,
born 'midst passionate rending of the Earth
fused by fires from Hades' searing depths,
rock piled on rock, screeching from natal pain,
then cooled, lay still, assumed a coat
of verdant texture where puff-balled creatures feed.
Between the steepling hills, on valley's floor
there toils a race of men who harvest 'neath the ground
black forests of prehistoric times,
great trees of yore, compressed
by frozen sheath, alluring, dangerous,
buried deep, black gold. Industry's food.
Ripped from stubborn beds in narrow caves,
cursed, attacked, bathed by sweaty toil
watched by eyes alert in old, grimed faces
for signs of treachery, collapse.
From resentful silent tunnels dark as night
o'er which no sun will ever rise
come roars from metal monsters, briefly - then silence.
Drip, drip, waters from a far-off world
filter to the coal-dust floor, footprints still
of miners; echoes of their voices fading,
Victims, crushed, airless, prisoners in stone
are memorials to Nature's implacable price,
whilst up above a land so wondrous fair, unaware
of suffering endured below its feet,
gazes from towering mountain peaks in pride
at all the grandeur, satisfied
in its snow-capped realm, remote,
placated by each human sacrifice.

'Do you have to go down the pit, our Da?'
Eyes look down, a working hand explores
the thick unruly hair with love.
'Indeed I must my son, for that is where we
earn our daily bread.'

Bruce Kennard-Simpson (Otterton)

A Friend

She's there when you need a helping hand
When you feel you are sinking in the sand,
When things just get so hard to do
She is always there for you.

You know she's there if you need to call
When you feel that you are going to fall.
She always says what you need to hear
Taking away some of the fear.

She will try her best to make you smile
Tell you to go that extra mile.
I know on her I can depend
My very, very special friend.

Annette Redwood (Torquay)

Autumn

So now the autumn to mists begin to rise
And darker clouds go hurrying through the skies
The autumn winds contest the summer breeze
Shaking the lustrous green leaves from the trees
Into yellow and to gold, a sight to see
A wondrous carpet in the woods for you and me
The misty autumn sun when day is done
Is Mother Nature's gift for everyone
Not to regret the passing of the summer days
For autumn is beautiful in many ways

Roma Court

Magpies And Magnolia

A tree-lined road where houses once spacious,
In days when living was truly gracious,
Now huddle together, extended
In a manner never intended
By the builders long ago.
Victorian gardens had to go.
Magnolia trees no longer bloom,
Car parking takes a lot of room.
Only the magpies fly around
Or strut about along the ground.
The canopied trees mere saplings then.
Now spread their shade to other men.

Margaret J Howes (Torquay)

What Will Be?

Only a man as old as me
Can see the world is ending
Because we never listen to
The message that I am sending

I speak and tell the world of
The knowledge I have learnt
All the books and things I've read
Are now destroyed or burnt

If only Man could learn to love
And follow all the laws
The world would be a happy place
No fighting and no wars

There is nothing I can do myself
Just follow what I've shown
Before the darker skies arrive
And leave us on our own

B A Gill (Ottery St Mary)

The Bristol Channel

Our house beside
A flowing tide,
A channel wide
Two coasts divide.

Welsh mountains high
Gold sunset sky
White seagulls fly
Cool sea breeze sigh.

Great ships afloat,
The Pilot's boat
Deep throbbing note
From engine's throat.

Night skies of stars
A glimpse of Mars
The lights of cars
Two bridges' spars.

With such a view
Forever new
God's love is true
For me and you.

Anne Golding (Portishead)

Summer In September

A symphony of starlings floating in the breeze
With auburn-coloured leaves drifting from the trees.
The Yorkshire Dales bathed in all its splendour
And a place we love in the summer of September.

Lost in our adventure in a dream, a cocoon,
Like the imaginary story of Lorna Doone.
From an open fire, logs crackling through the fender
On a lazy evening in the summer of September.

Dry stone walls and round pebble pots,
Yorkshire pudding and goosegogs with clots.
As blue and yellow are mixed to make green,
The beauty of the Earth and the sky can be seen.

Can you hear the soft music in what you see?
Can you feel the beauty of the soul that's free?
When did you last feel this way, can you remember?
Was it last year - in the summer of September?

G Jones (Plymouth)

The Sleeper

Wood pigeon softly cooed
the mind quiet for a while
of the demons that bubble
under a complacent lid of calm.

The old beech tree smiles down
waving a cool green serenity
over a puce-tinted sky.

Looking up in awe of its strength
I am distracted by the beetles scuttling
over the peeling skin to feast greedily.

Penetrating the soft juicy core
it docs not complain.

Only the wind takes up a protest
to mourn for its pain.

I dare to touch the rough-hewn hide
but sharp spelks of pain
pierce my wooden heart.

The branch above gives a sickening crack
the wind has won this battle.
The beetles pour forth and I wake up.

Julie Hubbard (Tiverton)

Twenty-Four

A Wetland sunrise, morning alight with gossamer threads.
Floating ethereal strands of radiance enhanced with dewy beads.
A flattened landscape, Heaven's gate, gouged with
symmetrical *rhines.
With creative splendour adorned.

Awesome, active, alive, under the warmth of a noon sun.
Palliative hues of iridescent lincoln.
Shimmering above the calmness of flight and hoof.
Creation's business being conducted.

Sky on fire as sunset looms, a bragging extravagant statement.
Roosting, settling, nature predictably compliant.
The net of evening squeezing colour and contour.
Darkness swallowing the land.

Splendid, majestic stars, atop the moor at midnight.
Clarity of sound, a revelation. Creation under moonlight.
Owning every inch of willow and reed.
Until, with the first finger of dawn,
The Wetlands turn, full circle.

Rhine . . . local word for a ditch.

Julia Smith (Langport)

Current Criticism

I've been around for ninety years;
Materially now better off.
The world I knew and loved, long gone,
Replaced by many common fears.

Climate; the point of no return?
Temperature rise, and water scarce.
Without some U-turns taken soon
Eventually we'll surely burn.

On diet 'eat more fish' the cry;
Advice that few would are gainsay.
But how? When seas are overfished
And trawled to leave such scant supply.

No progress then sans education.
Britain's suffering constant change.
Returning to some old and tried
Could be in time to save our nation.

We're in this world to make things good.
Not always gazing towards Heaven.
Less alcohol, more exercise and sleep,
And for our youngsters, better food.

Today we cherish 'Nanny State'.
Good in parts, a loophole for greed.
More self-reliance is the key
To progress at a faster rate.

Employment rat race too intense,
Many needing to slow down.
Basics all too oft ignored.
What became of common sense?

Don Bishop (Highbridge)

On Reaching Seventy-Five

I often dreamed in childhood how I'd reach the highest road,
But living life was oh so hard, I never reached that goal.
Through many years of striving for somewhere, somehow or when,
Those days are gone but dreams still come to taunt me now and then.
But now I find a way through things,
The way we all should follow,
Be content with what we have, look forward to tomorrow.
As I look back I now recall the blessings and the good times,
That hand in hand went with my dreams throughout this life of mine.
I never climbed that highest mountain, never played on golden sands,
Never held a glowing sunset in the hollow of my hand,
But I saw the lovely country, the flowers, birds and trees,
The children and their innocence and am content with these.

Molly Buckland (Wiltshire)

Living Here

You hear it in the waves that lap the shore
and in the lark's song, high above the moor
and in the blissful quiet of woodland shade;
the owl's hoot as the light begins to fade.

You see it as the lambs dance in the spring
and hazel catkins tremble on a string
from trees just bursting into leaf
to shade the primrose-covered banks beneath.

You smell it in the bluebell-covered glade
and in the cottage garden, where parade
sweet lavender and rosemary and thyme
and roses rambling in a riot, quite sublime.

You feel it as the sea mist stalks the coast
and swirls your sum of senses in a host
of pleasurable sensation that the best
of life, is to be found in the South West.

Brenda Heath (Torquay)

The Willow Tree

The willow tree her branches bare,
Overlooked a country garden.
Bird tables and fresh water there
As winter weather hardened.

Grey squirrels leapt from bough to bough,
Assessing peanuts suspended,
Then crawled along the clothes line
To break bags and eat upended.

Screeching starlings spooked to flight
Sped to the willow's sanctuary
Thus startling cooing collared doves
To join them in the spreading tree

A mouse whose hole was at the base
Darted for titbits relinquished
Much too soon for robin redbreast
Whose high hopes were soon extinguished.

A woodpecker drilled into the bark
Exposing insects hiding there
Its rapid tattoo echoing
Throughout the frosty air.

A blackbird feeding on the ground,
Paused and chattered out a warning,
Flying for refuge in the tree
As a cat was seen marauding.

Blue tits, blackcaps and finches galore
All welcome in the willow's arms,
When danger threatens up they soar
Safe from predatory alarms.

Doreen Barnes (Exeter)

Summer 2006

It's the hottest day of the year; in fact
it's the hottest July day on record.
I've opened doors and windows, but a trapped fly,
lost in its own artless world, is still knocking its head
on the bathroom skylight, in a vain attempt to reach clear blue sky.
Suddenly there's an almighty bang.
It could so easily have been a bomb,
but it's just the wind slamming the back door.
On the back lawn, in the scorching sunshine,
a jackdaw's lying with both wings outstretched.
From above it looks like a Stealth bomber waiting for a signal to
get airborne.
As I turn towards the stairs, there's a thud in the hall.
It could have been a missile, but it's just the glossy pages
of a mail order catalogue, inviting you
to buy things which you can't really afford.

Outside, in the cottage garden, the air is laden
with the scent of old-fashioned roses,
their full heads balanced between maturity and decay.
The jackdaws are back in their hangars, the bees busy serving
their queen.
Further down the garden, I find the carcass of a small goldfinch.
These days you can't rule out bird flu,
but it's more likely the work of our neighbour's cat.
Long after sunset I go out to lock the garage.
There's no moon. The wind has dropped and the last bat has
deserted the sky.
In the distance, way across the meadows,
I can hear the dying rattle of a train.
Now it's nearly midnight, and the air's cool.
There's nothing but silence and pitch darkness.
This could be the end of the world,
but it's just the end of another day.

Keith Shaw (Templecombe)

A-Time Honoured Cruise

(To the Isles of Scilly from Penzance)

The ship's whistle blows as astern she goes,
Scillonian-III moves so gently.
She comes about on a beautiful day,
another trip is underway.
She sails along the coast so clear,
with all and everyone in good cheer.

As we head across the deep blue sea,
some dolphins alongside make special company,
Up and down in the surf they play,
to one and all making everyone's day

On the horizon the islands we see,
soon we'll appreciate their tranquillity.
As we dock at St Mary's quay,
the passengers wait with great curiosity.
The gangway secure they go on their way,
enjoying the sun, as for a while they stay.

'Tis four o'clock, the ship's whistle blows,
another half hour and away she goes,
We sail down through Crow, the island's aglow,
the passengers gazing with wondrous awe.

We leave the islands in the evening breeze,
the passengers relaxed and all at ease,
We pass the Wolf Rock on our starboard side,
as over the sea we seem to glide.
Soon we are off the mainland again
as, through the years, we pass Land's End -
the time-honoured saying, 'We must come again'.

Another trip over and all's been plain sailing,
as the passengers take their last view, from the ship's railing.

N C Grenfell (Penzance)

The Day Of The Sun

From east to west
The sun, in all his glory
Drives his chariot down the ever-changing sky.
His path is sure and at noon's height
Looks down on landscape bright
With hedges, fields and streams.
Cattle and sheep graze lazily in the afternoon haze
That goes on and cools to eventide.
The birds twitter as home they fly.
Dusk descends, and they are safely in the nest.
The sun, now firmly in the west
Spreads the sky with colours of every hue
And sinks, in glorious orange, purple, red and blue.

Doris Mary Miller (Wellington)

Second Marriage At Max Gate

She sits alone in a room of another's choice:
Above her, that other's picture gazing down
In a silent condemnation; no single voice
To answer her own.

For the famous man of letters she married with pride
Sits mewed in his study, with mind turned back to a time
Shared with a woman once loved, who has left his side,
But lives in his rhyme.

Too late his genius commends her, so long since gone.
In his memory sounds her youthful voice, low-calling.
Through the windows, the empty fields, their harvest done;
And the rain falling.

Betty M Harris (Taunton)

This Land Of Mine

I laid down on sacred ground
With clay beneath my head. I
Wanted to refresh my mind, but
I had a dream instead. I may
Have a weird awaken but I
Will understand. As I lay here
On the surface of what is now
A peaceful land. I hold faith
And trust in thee. You have
Always filled my mind. I
Carry what is no burden and
Will always look back with
Pride. You are my home. You
Are my land I can now
Reach out and touch thee with
What is now a feeble hand. This
Hand I place upon my brow
And with land beneath my
Feet. I promise they will be forever
A place for you in me. The not so
Good things have been and gone.
The good things passed by too.
Now deep in my heart and
Soul there will always
Be a place for you.

Richard Mahoney (Lancing)

Spring Miracle

Suddenly it's all happening!
Cherry trees in bunched pinks and reds
Magnolias in full bloom.
Fruit blossoms in brilliant white plumes.
A floral fireworks display!
Tree leaves all unfurled,
Fir cones shining in the sun,
Fountains of yellow broom:
Joyful surge of life.
Every thing is happy!
Summer just around the corner
From this late spring
And it's all happened
In the last few days!
Wow!

John M Cox (Crowborough)

Heytesbury

Here in the Wylye Valley
The village of Heytesbury stands
With ancient church and roofs of thatch
And gardens bright and grand.

The villagers enjoy the beauty all around
They walk their dogs for miles and miles
Over the plain and up the hills
Through gates and fields and over stiles.

And I, with Martha, full of fun
Go on our daily trek.
See squirrels, rabbits and the deer
Beside the rippling beck.

It fills my mouth with songs of praise
And thanks to God above
For all the beauty here around
But most of all His love.

Eileen Smith (Heytesbury)

The Children's Dance At Helston

We'll dance in the dawn and through the blue day,
We'll dance like the stars in the wild, whirling spray
Away on curled waves as they surge up the bay.

We'll dance in the morning when the sun rises high
To the whisper of leaves as the wind rustles by
And the larks pour their song on the earth from the sky.

Then down the cool gardens through noon's blazing hours,
Where fountains fall splashing in cold diamond-showers
And freshen the faces of sweet-scented flowers.

We are the children who dance like the light
Dressed as the moon is in silvery white,
Frocks fashioned from stars on a fine summer night.

We'll skip through dew till the thin mists rise
And the glow-worm lamps burn green, and the skies
Deepen, rose-gold, as the daylight dies.

We'll fade like pale flowers, and turn into dreams
Caught in the gleam of the moon's magic beams
As they shatter on glass of deep pools and dark streams.

When gales come and winter, sad earth wrapped in grey,
In a numb, frozen silence we stay hidden away;
But we'll dance through the spring on the first shining day.

Diana Momber (Falmouth)

Suns May Shine

It's your birthday tomorrow, and we've bickered again,
Neither seems able to count to ten - rattling dishes, slamming doors,
'It's your turn to walk the dog,' - 'No yours!'
Nothing's too trivial for us to fight,
Now, I have your card to write.
We're having one of our silences, that usually follow our spats,
So how can I send you this rubbish, when we've just fought like cats,
The card says, you're the best in the world, of course that isn't true,
You're cranky, and difficult, yet no silly card, can tell of my love for you,
For after the quarrels, that some never have, do they miss out
                                                    on the rose?
The making up - loving - and after the loving the web, of the afterglow.
I hope that suns may shine on you, not just on your birthday,
But all of your tomorrows' suns; shine on you, lighting your way.
I won't sign with kisses, we're not speaking as yet, but there will
                                                    be no surprise,
We'll giggle, and our hands will touch, and we'll love again, just with
                                                    our eyes - tomorrow.

R Cole (Plymouth)

Ode To The Eden Project

In Cornwall lies the jewel of Eden,
Where plants enjoy their jungled freedom.
The desert of the china clay
Has bloomed like night turned into day.
The challenge of regeneration
Has resurrected God's creation.
Beneath the vast white bubble wrap,
It nestles in the white gold gap
Of Austell's wasted wilderness.
New vision's been born, a heaven no less.
A microcosm of the world,
From mighty tree to fern unfurled;
Green heartbeat of the world's revealed
By waving palms to paddy field.
Stand and feel the humid tropic,
Where growth is rapid, flowers exotic;
Plants for shelter, bamboo huts
Surrounded by fruit, berries, nuts.
Cascades of water tumble down
The steep cliffs from the biome's crown.
Come to Eden's temperate zone,
Where citrus vibrant colour's shown.
Their fragrance and fecundity
Show God gives food abundantly;
And we're reliant on each other
To conserve for sister, brother
This world of beauty beyond all price:
God's gift to us, Earth's paradise.

Janet Lang (Seaton)

Shedding Skin . . .

departs another day
farewell
my pure Isolde
kiss and tell
by eve's end tarnished
no dried morning dew
sun-rising 'morrow's
chance anew

fond-waving bids
past-hours brave
to kneel before
our restless wave
seeing out the past
and all man's folly
disbanding lonely
heart's life melancholy

set the sun
with fresh desire
reach out, slide free
of coarse quagmire
for optimistic view
prevails
and insignificant
ignorance fails

from daylight shadows
circumspect
sheds brooding whispers
into hope's effect
transmogrified
though often torn
from angst-tapped chrysalis
to free-flying newborn

Jamie Caddick (Bristol)

Holsworthy, Devon

In Holsworthy town
The roads go up and down.
Though the town is small
The churches stand tall.
I'm happy to say
Wednesday's still market day.
You'll find when you're there
That The Square's just not square:
It's not rectangular,
But is triangular.
There are no trains today,
Beeching took them away,
But you can see for miles,
That is great cause for smiles.
You can see Dartmoor,
The church on Brentor,
And quite a lot more.

Catherine Blackett (Holsworthy)

Ilfracombe

'B & B' and 'Vacancies'.
The pleading signs proclaim,
From terraces once elegant
And hopefully spruced again,
With windows bright and gardens neat
And a seductive name.
But round the corner, up the hill
Where windows should contain

A potted fern or china dog
In dim and lace-fringed bay,
The hi-fi thumps past grubby panes
And littered flaking doors.
The tonsured gardens on 'the front'
Municipally gay
Have seats and slopes and shelters
For the out-of -season tours

Of coaches from the Midlands full of
Girlish OAPs
Cut-price, close-pursed and skittish, but
The season's at an end,
And the young are dole-queue drifters
Who busk and loll at ease.
Carefree, careless, tho' colourful
They stay, but never spend.

Midst 'Devon Teas' and empty shops
And 'gifts' and 'closing sales',
With trips to Lundy, Exmoor scenes
And 'area relief'
The high street fights to woo the crowds
To Devon's craggy North, but fails
To cure a telly-tutored taste
For Tenerife!

P C Pool (Ilfracombe)

Orchestra St Eustachius Church, Tavistock

A huge fortissimo
crashes its climactic chords
down crowded aisles
out into June dusk

the audience
part of a pulsating whole
transfixed
absorbed by music
at one with the building
the walls and pillars
containing this
uncontainable resonance

then
the fade to pianissimo
tension lifts
listeners relax
separate to individuals
wrapped and cosseted
in gentle melody

the finale
satisfied applause
dream-like the audience
strengthened
refreshed
drifts into gathering night
tipped back
into the humdrum world

Jacqui Fogwill (Tavistock)

Devon

A county named from its natural ore
With sandstone cliffs and pebbled shores,
Its green surpasses all throughout
This pleasant land.
Landscape's beauty does steal all eyes
From pastures elsewhere espied,
Revealing historical features
Of this unique isle.
Hidden caves along a coastal line
Where smugglers found solace for a time,
And treasures ne'er to be found.
The beaches of sand and stone
Where many in the summer roam,
And others in the sun's rays
Enjoy a tan for many days.
There is nothing to compare
With what Devon has to share.

D R Thomas (Ottery St Mary)

Passing Girl

After your departure I perceived it
as *hegira,* your flight to safety
from whatever threatened you here.
Yet your timing seemed callous
so soon after your birthday gift:
sun and fun, on African safari,
tracking and trekking, me so blind to
your unease even when together under canvas.
You endured our campfire sundowners,
a leopard's cough, elephants rumbling.
In the bush we were captive companions
until our return to city life and
your surprise elision with a new love.

Angst left me listening to your absence,
resonant routines and rites of past communion,
your contralto cadence in the bath,
that telephone tittle-tattle with
phantom friends and colleagues; your
muzzling charm that deferred our disputes.
Sometimes we lay beneath a duvet,
the dawn chorus replacing semantics,
such rare accord over spot-the-birdsong.
How daintily you dipped bare toes into
the green cataracts of our stair carpet,
you and the house mouse both so
methodical, I once dared to tease.

You were the fast in breakfast, just pecking,
whereas I devoured food, more gourmand than gourmet.
You stripped kitchen suds from your wrists
while I dried the crockery, you said,
'Like a lion with a lute!'

I complain to the hollowness in vain,
wilderness reaching my door again.

Malcolm Williams (Cheltenham)

Bully

That's what you are, you're just a bully
I want you to understand that fully
You punch and pinch, torment and tease
Push and pull, bring me to my knees
You bruise, scratch and mentally scar
Just who do you think you really are?
You're making me sad, affecting my health
I'm becoming a shadow of my former self
But I've had enough, I won't let you beat me
I won't let your fists and comments defeat me
I'm going to make sure this doesn't worsen
I'm going to become the stronger person
I'll tell someone how you make me suffer
Someone whose resolve for change will be tougher
With that person's help, I will go far
In showing you up as the worm that you are
You will shrink, my esteem will grow stronger
And I will be fearful of you no longer.

Paul Spender (Bridgwater)

No Names, No Pack Drills

I pick up my calls and utter my spiel
Then answer my callers who've had a rough deal.
For some it's graffiti, that's scrawled on their wall
While others, fly-tipping, to trip on and fall.

Trees that hold steadfast on pavement and roof
Cars left abandoned or dumped on the hoof
Recycled boxes and waste stand unclaimed,
And all sorts of litter get kicked down my lane!

I smile to my back teeth, say, 'All will be well'
Until I get nabbed by my caller from Hell.

I sigh as I humble, bent down on one knee
To hear at you barrack and barrage your plea
So I let my mind wander to sand and blue sea
And ponder at people no different than me.

That their tiny problems are blown out of sinc
Today, have you sat to proportion and think?

Life's tiny treasures are seldom, unseen
They harbour a notion, concealed, like a dream.
The good things, the bad things, though tangled and frayed
For in their small package their balance is weighed

That all life's small problems are gifts in disguise
To trade with and bargain at no one's demise.

So next time you mouth off to argue the toss
Rethink your blessings and see who is boss.
And don't let life's hiccups commit your display
But laugh at life's treasures as they come your way.

So I should be grateful, when closing my call
That I haven't ventured to taking that fall.

Frances Johnson (Swindon)

Petals Unfurled

At birth, a tightly-closed bud
Waiting to be nourished,
From the brain's tangled growth
Until the seed has flourished.

A personality is formed,
Descriptions put on file,
Each blossom has a name,
Many questions bring a smile.

A bouquet of knowledge gained,
The flower is opened wide,
Fed with information
Our reflection is inside.

J Carter (Taunton)

My Town In South Devon

I live alone at the top of a hill
The third terrace up from the town
There are beautiful views, right over the bay
A lot of hills going up and then down
There are 50 steps down, 'Queen's Steps' to the road
And 50 more down to the quay
Five minutes more, and I'm right near the shops
I can walk or bus home, with my load
There is town, harbour, marina and beach
All within 10 minutes from home
A lot of people come on holiday here
Because everywhere is within reach
The coastal path is not very far
- It leads right round to Kingswear
Around five headlands, it is nine miles
I could not walk back, so, go by car
The town of . . . lies on the east coast
Of a buttress that, juts out at the sea
'We're' a peninsula here, it's called Berryhead
- A French garrison had played the last post.

Jane H M Hudson

Portholland

There's nothing at Portholland
And *that* is its attraction,
Just sea and sand and sky and cliffs -
No modern-day distraction.

The shop was closed last summer.
Its chapel's been converted;
The river's man-made waterfall
To natural green's reverted.

The cliffs are bathed in sunshine
In summer-clothed perfection
Of pale pink Thrift on slate grey rock
Against sky-blue reflection

There's 'nothing' at Portholland
If that means man's invention;
Yet, truly, it has everything
Of Nature's pure intention.

Sheila Fermor Clarkson (St Austell)

Loving Choice

You really do have to be hopelessly in love
to *be happily married*. Without being cynical -
it happens. When very young my bicycle was
my love, *(as I then understood)*.
Then as I grew older, there entered my life
an additional love - my darling Grace.
How fortunate I was to be able to come to the
correct decision, that first love had to
recede into a happy memory, realising that
bicycles *respond to care,* but do not
reciprocate true love, that led to marriage
and everlasting companionship.
There's a wonder I feel sometimes, of not
knowing, that if a bicycle has not been for me
in the first place, how differently my future
might have been - that is, of course, *hypothetically!*
I thank the Lord, for the one memory to
treasure, *(and the best of all),* a dear wife forever.

John Cole (Swindon)

The Gift

(For Rachel)

What can I do
to thank you for your love?
If I were God
I'd hang a million stars
along each bone
of your bright body.

I would give you
moons for breasts
to send your brilliance
streaming through the night.
I'd set a sun
to blaze between your thighs.

Alas, I am not God!
And so I give
these fragile lines.
And then I offer you
my self.

Richard Henry (Cheltenham)

Brimpsfield - My Village

In deepest, darkest Gloucestershire,
Among the wolds and wealds,
On high ground in the Cotswolds,
Lies a hamlet called Brimpsfield,
Not many people live here,
No post office, pub or shop,
It lies upon the Cotswold hills,
Right on the very top,
It's cold here in the winter,
With lots and lots of snow,
And open to the elements,
We feel the north wind blow,
In winter, it's a cold, dark place,
With rain and hail to sting your face,
The cottages are made of stone,
Around in winter, the cold winds moan.
In summer, it is a different place, we smell the new-mown hay,
Warm sunshine, peace, a perfect place to spend the day,
There is an ancient Norman church
With graves so very old.
Giffard has a battle here, so often I've been told
Alas the castle stands no more the moat has long run dry,
Above high in the trees, the rooks give mournful cry,
A small black pump stands by the fields
Alas no water now it yields,
A house stands where the school once stood.
The lane winds down to the snowdrop wood,
Brimpsfield is a very nice place to live
And has many, many pleasures to give.

Elizabeth Woodham (Brimpsfield, Gloucester)

All Hallows Eve

Hallowe'en, and nearly dark along the path
Around the trees, a short cut, well used
In the day, but silent and forbidding now
As the last light drains away.

The tall firs like a menace loom,
Throwing down a deeper gloom.
Stillness as a cover lies below
The cloud-filled, starless skies.

Quiet movements from behind
Tip the balance of the mind,
Advancing on the gravelled ground
Within the minimum of sound.

Panic, like a lightning bolt restricts
The chest and numbs the throat.
An atom of primeval fear
Whispers to the straining ear,
'What entity progresses there,
Displacing stones, disturbing air,
Upon the ride that skirts the trees.
Early, on All Hallows Eve?'

Betty Duberley (Ruardean)

'Crufts' Thoughts In The Ring

The confidence of ignorance, is that a foolish thing,
Or the hesitancy of knowledge, when you're standing in the ring.
You know you have a good dog, you know he fits the bill
But does the judge know just as well, or will the score be nil?
You look at all the other dogs, and think, *I should have first.*
Oh hurry up and finish the class, I've got one hell of a thirst.
When I first started showing dogs, dot-dot years ago
I really thought I had the goods, but little did I know.
But now I have the knowledge of the standard of the collie
Look at the judge just standing there, what a flipping Wally.
Hang on a bit! I've got the first, oh he's a super man
I always knew he knew his stuff, now I'm his biggest fan.

Flora Denning (Berkeley)

Find The Child

Find the child within you.
It's there, inside your mind,
And even though the years have passed,
It's not been left behind.

Remember how it used to be
When you weren't very big?
The wonder of a flower,
Or the magic of a twig?

To run, just for the joy of it,
To skip across the grass.
To watch some tiny insect
As the quiet minutes pass.

To sit, with mind, wide open,
Absorbing all around.
Quite bereft of toil or worry,
Where tranquillity is found.

We've forgotten how to do it
As the short years sped away.
But you can find it, if you want to,
You can bring back yesterday.

Regain that sense of wonder,
Amazed by all you see.
The universe, spread out before you,
Imagination let run free.

But don't neglect your duties!
That path only leads to strife.
But, for a moment, be a child again,
And restore your faith in life!

Johne Makin (Plymouth)

May On Wye

On cushioned turf
I sat alone.
My back against
the sun-hot stone.
I breathed the breeze
Of middle May,
All pollen-rich,
That sunwashed day.

I smelled the blossom,
Scanned the sky.
A pigeon cooed
Across the Wye.
A cuckoo called,
Faint, sweet, benign.
That afternoon
At Bredwardine . . .

Donald Harris (Lydney, Gloucestershire)

Ashton Court's Nature

As I walked into the beautiful park,
I witnessed shades of brown changing light to dark.
The cloudless sky sweeping grey to blue,
Tree to tree the small birds flew.

Surrounded by different shades of green,
Lincoln light and dark hues were seen.
Creamy pink blossom tainted emerald trees,
Bush stood low with copper beech leaves.

Walking towards green open land,
A khaki tree with a sandy hand.
The fingers creeping trying to escape,
Rounded white clouds he tries to take.

In the woods you can clearly hear,
The chirps and shrills from far and near.
The giant pins are tall-standing pines,
Rising from cushions in parallel lines.

Stood up tall like a giant mast,
The distorted tree scarred by the past.
Damned and blackened with scar tissue,
Alone and abandoned this damaged yew.

The sadness of forgotten bluebells,
New beginnings like curled up tails.
Rich iron paths of treaded soft dirt,
The worn down tracks sweeping round to skirt.

Eleanor Smith (Bristol)

Yesterday

When we were young we used to play
In the fields of fresh-mown hay.
The ricks were built so straight and tall
We loved to jump upon them all.
The farmer then would shout at us
We wondered why he made a fuss.
He'd chase us then off of his land
A great big stick held in his hand.
Running fast up to the stile
We scramble o'er and pause a while.
Thinking we might catch a frog
We'd wander down into the bog.
Sinking into squelching mud
Forgot we promised to be good.
Off would come our socks and shoes
And into the water we'd dip our toes.
Although it didn't look to clean
We'd paddle off into the stream.
We'd find an old discarded tin
To catch some little tiddlers in.
Back onto the bank again
We'd saunter down the leafy lane.
Alas! the sun would be going down
We'd have to hurry back to town
The curfew rang always at eight
When we were young we daren't be late.
We had to be in bed by nine
Summer - winter, all the time.

PS
Now the kids aren't free to roam
They have to stay in sight of home
What happened to the days of yore?
That they can't roam as once before.

Pat Adams (Cheltenham)

Hymn To Dalmahra

In raiment of beech leaves and bryony, cowslip-shod,
She comes - our mother, our sister - by meadow and wood;
With the light in her eyes she kindles the lamp in the leaf
And the golden flames of the grasses
    Flicker and flare as she passes.

Clouds of bright butterflies burst from the lips of her laughter;
The echoing valleys she seeds with a song
    And the birds follow after -
Blackbird and nightingale, mistlethrush, robin and wren;
Wasteland and wilderness, places neglected of men,
She favours with flowers - trefoil, tendril and spray -
Un-numbered the blossoms, the blooms, she lets fall
    From her fragrant bouquet.

She hallows the watery places: midden and quag
She candles with asphodel, loosetrife, lily and flag;
The hithering, thithering bees are her brothers-in-love
For she suckles with honey the harebell, the heath
    And the velvet foxglove.

She moulds with her cloud-white hands the hills and the hollows;
With dew-light she dapples the dawn;
    She dresses the water with willows,
Embroiders the shadowy places, dingle and dell,
With violet, anemone, stitchwort and cool moschatel
To make for the elves a home in her Queendom of Leaves:
Let there be laughter and joy in the wake
    Of the dances she weaves.

Anthony Watts (Taunton)

Inside My Head

Inside my head
The voices are talking.
I hear them all the time.
They're even helping me
With this rhyme.
Why won't they shut up talking?
They won't shut up talking
Because they say they are real.
Why don't they understand
How bad they are making me feel?
The voices inside my head
Are helping me;
But I want to be free
The voices say
I will be free one day;
They have even said what day.
I want them to go now,
But to get them out of my head
I do not know how.
Please make the voices go away,
I do not want them to stay.

L J Casey (Plymouth)

Devon

If I had a song to sing
I'd sing of my life in Devon.
Of how this beautiful county
Could even be taken for Heaven.

I would sing of leafy lanes
And the place where the rivers meet.
Of long shadows and golden sunsets
Cooling slowly from earlier heat.

My song now becomes a chorus
As the rivers race down from the moor.
Forest trees would sway and bow
To flowers stretching up from the floor.

The peaceful sight of a single swan,
The shimmering sun a golden sphere.
Ripples spread as a kingfisher dives,
Grazing nearby, a herd of deer.

My song becomes a haunting one
As midnight chases the gold
Artistic strokes of yellow and red
Another song is about to unfold.

Barry Winters (Chudleigh)

Conflict

Roaring, ice-cold, loud splashing waterfalls
Vivid yellow buttercups spread over green field.
White daisies running free to woodland,
Ablaze with bluebells, wild creatures call.

Rain, soft hissing on brown barren earth,
Sprout strong stems, red poppies emerge.
Autumn riches, hedgerows, trees different hues.
Vigorous spring nudge nature to birth.

Designed by unseen hand,
the world creator.

Fires, destruction, war-torn lands, starvation.
Broken bodies, unseeing eyes stare upwards.
Oil spillage, choking pain, dying birds.
Forest attacked by acid pollution, uncaring nation.

Hunters stalk, destroy life motivated by greed.
Unemployed, street-begging, building raised to ground.
Busy large cities, symbolic high-tower offices,
Progress fashionably, ignore homeless, desperate need.

Destructive selfish blinked man,
the world breaker.

Phyllis Smith (Weston-Super-Mare)

Spring

Awakening senses
Wilderness teeming with life,
Every kind of life
And promise here.
Immensity of colour and movement
Under the hand of Spring.
Blue bands across the valley
White clouds overhead
A soft breeze blowing,
Daisies in the wet lush grass.
Sunshine and cloud,
Pleasant birdsong
In the air.
Nothing discordant,
Peace, perfect peace.
Daffodils swaying
In the March wind.
Primulas and primroses,
Peeping out
In the gentle sun
Robin, finch and thrush
Singing their hearts out.
The air is clear
The view is bright.
Some smoke from chimneys
Curling and swirling free
In the breeze.
Oh! Clear, calm day,
Peace, perfect peace.
Here one could almost
Reach out and touch
The living silence
And catch one's breath
Feel its gentle healing touch
Peace, perfect peace.

P Laing (Taunton)

Nature

Nature is so lovely with bird and beast and flower;
Brightly coloured plumage; fur glossy, groomed and sleek;
Blossoms, petals glowing in sunshine and in shower;
Mountain rising splendid, brook, valley, sea and creek.

Nature is so cruel. Scared prey no mercy finding,
Creature hunting creature with talon, tooth and claw.
Victims claimed by hunger die daily, each reminding
Of struggles for survival. Nature in the raw.

Nature has four seasons. In Spring green buds are showing.
Summer's scented gardens bring singing birds and bees.
Autumn's coloured pageant has reds and coppers glowing.
Winter's wet and fogbound, or white with snowy trees.

Nature is a mother for all creation caring,
Pleasant things or horrid in each a purpose find.
If only everyone could learn the art of sharing
Nature's balanced planning could benefit mankind.

Jean Perkins (Salisbury)

A Devon November

I walked to the top of the hill today,
And the sea in the distance was misty blue,
And the wind sang in the cedar trees,
A sighing, soughing symphony for autumn.

Oak leaves skittered in a golden shower
And the sycamores rustled, whispering softly,
While deep in the bank by the chestnut tree
Hidden snowdrops slept, dreaming of spring.

Two magpies scolded high in the hawthorn hedge,
Gleaming feathers ruffled, and a tiny wren
Quested in the lower branches, tail skyward,
Pert, alert, bright of eye.

Sparrows gossiped in a sheltered corner
Warmed by a slanted sunbeam in the blackthorn,
And a little ginger cat, the colour of the season,
Chased his tail in a rustle of brown beech leaves.

Autumn sang this morning on the hill:
A farewell to the swallow and the sun,
A greeting to the wild geese, reclaiming the estuary,
A sonnet in sound for a Devon November.

Chrys Aitken (Bideford)

Cornwall's Magic

High on the cliffs, the seagulls soar,
Riding the thermals, above the ocean's roar.
Yellow-headed gorse, candytuft, and rosy thrift,
Like a carpet spread, to give your spirits a lift.

Derelict chimneys, like cathedrals stand,
Relics of the days, when men gouged the land.
Singing the words of a John Wesley hymn,
While the land gave up its treasure of tin.

Myths and magic, and Celtic folklore,
Smugglers have hidden around its rocky shore.
Watching and waiting, for ships to come to grief,
As well they did, on many a reef.

Quaint little harbours, and lighthouses that blink,
It makes you want to stop and think, of,
The trawlers and fishermen, who ply their trade, and
Cornish brass bands, and the steam engines that parade.

Church bells, and chapels, a way of life,
The WI run by a farmer's wife.
Tourists come in their thousands to see,
The sands, the surf, and power of the sea,
And, the magic, that Cornwall holds for me.

Anne Roberts (Plymouth)

Verse Versus Verse

In our dear land there was a time
    when those composing verse
took pains each line should scan and rhyme
        and if lines didn't rhyme and scan
        conforming to some favoured plan
        they'd start again where they began
    (no doubt they'd also curse!)

Thus Chaucer and thus Spenser wrote
    and this was Shakespeare's choice
(in sonnets not in plays, please note)
        and Dryden's - Laureate the first.
        And Keats', for long cool'd draught a-thirst,
        and countless poets, all well-versed
    and Betjeman's loved voice.

But those there are who write not thus
    composing verse - but 'free'.
Is formal writing needless fuss?
        Do rules restrict spontaneous thought
        Does verse that rhymes amount to naught?
        Is free verse an ideal long sought?
    Will somebody tell me.

So are the free verse writers right
    their notebooks thus to fill?
Is theirs true poetry, despite
        six hundred years of rhyme concern?
        Are modernists correct to spurn
        an art-form they won't stoop to learn?
    - Or do they lack the skill?

Martin Summers (Crediton)

Highland Holiday

Autumn cold winds blow keenly again,
Chilling the evening air.
Patterns of sunshine play on the lawn
While daytime still lurks there.
Summer is nearly over and we recall its delight.
The mind reverts to Black Isle country,
Lochs and mountains; and beautiful sight
Of dolphins sporting at sea.

Along little lanes hide the secrets of glens,
Heather-clad, luscious and green-
Twisting paths twirling through pretty wild flowers,
Waterfalls cascading downstream.
Flat rocks by rivers forming, a seat upon which to gaze
On kingfishers, flashing and swooping in flight,
Small fish slinking onwards. picked out by sun's rays
And damsel flies shimmering so bright.

The villages all have their own special charm,
Spread out round a small market place.
Quaint, antique cottages within narrow streets,
Old windows adorned with fine lace.
Each tells a story of old-fashioned doings in centuries past,
No gas and electrics, but candles and fire,
Warm family life, and affections which last
Between children and mother and sire.

Castles and churches make history alive
From all the fine kings to this day.
To visit these places indeed is a pleasure,
Or view them the televised way.
On the main road in our village, there stands a large church and hall,
So Och had a jolly service on Sunday
With friendly welcome to one and all.
The sun shone its best on holiday.

A Audrey Agnew (Yeovil)

Plant Will Grow Again

You see people in the south-west
Watching waves of water at the beach
And can see birds flying around.
Their emotions and happiness are not negative things
But positive things.
Local fields going over to building sites in times of need.
They're strong in persons to sit and listen for support
It's like a plant growing again.
But when the wildlife in the south-west
Lift yourself for a loud boost
If it means to be just down to happiness
Strong positive people, its like lifting things cannot be
a replacement for things you lose.
But the plant will grow again.

Tina Sandford (Exeter)

Two Famous Places

Plymouth Hoe - where Drake played bowls;
Saw Spain's Armada come;
Little ships with Devon men,
Like hornets attacked tall galleons,
And not unaided
Put Spain's fleet to flight
Guided by the winds of God
'He blew with his winds
And they were scattered'
So says, the memorial on Plymouth Hoe.

Exeter with famed cathedral
Late Gothic's, perfect work.
There stressed people may be calmed
By its atmosphere of holy peace
You who are troubled
Come feel God's presence there.
You who are troubled come feel
The centuries of worship and prayer
Bringing peace to stressed folk today.

Frances Joan Tucker (Exmouth)

Cornwall

Mystic Celtic days of old
Ghosts of times gone by
Memories and wondrous signs
Seen both in earth and sky
Old castles, witches, wizards too
And knights of old on quests untold
In Cornwall passing through

This special part of History
And places kept in time
Tells of magic spells and mystery
Part of your life maybe and mine
Past and present, future too
All the signs to prove them true.

B P Willetts (St Austell)

Winter

Time steps up a gear as though racing to the Spring,
Anxious in case life never starts over again.
I hate the dark mornings, the dark evenings,
The dark recesses of my soul where depression lurks ready to
                                                    engulf me.
Deep, long, dark days, hardly light at noon,
A few snatched short hours of freedom,
Before blackness closes in once more.
Chilled winds wait round corners to ambush, push and hold,
Then let go, leaving me unbalanced, vulnerable.
Black ice lurks. Slush lingers, darkening like a rug inside
                                                    busy hallways,
Dampness fills the air, cloys my hair and rots my bones.
It's like living in a fog.
I watch the clocks, turn up the heat, and wear more layers.
Eat suet puddings, chips and cakes, then wrapped in blubber,
                                                    flounder like a seal,
Until shuffled under the covers I envy the tortoise, the bear, the
                                                    slumbering toad.
I'm awake but my soul is hibernating.
Leave me be.
Wake me up when it's springtime again.

Linda Lewis (Paignton)

Memories Of Cornwall

How steep and rough
The path we climbed
To se the beauty
Now left behind

Below lies footprints
Upon spacious sand
Washed by the sea
Touched by our hands

My eyes still see you
Tall, standing there
Arms outstretched
Wind blowing your hair

Soon once again
The path I'll see
And travel it full
Of memories.

Elizabeth Cowley-Guscott (Bristol)

Peace In The Coalfield

Where the whirring of the pulley
Or the metallic grate of the aerial flight?
Where the precious black gold
Unceremoniously ripped from this verdant pasture?

Twenty years have idled by, since last we stood on this spot,
Now the silence is broken only by
The crashing of the endless tide
And the cries of the voracious birds resting on the cliffs.

Yet yonder rests a man-made hill made from slag and waste,
And a beach still black as the cormorant that has returned to nest.
The lift shaft wheel now a decorative symbol,
Where a worker can fill his cup with yesterday.

No longer do men trudge in line down the street,
Dragging their feet to their next shift;
Their 'bait' tucked firmly under their arms
Dreading the weary, wet and wasted hours ahead.

For here today lies the bruised remains of a once vociferous giant,
Heralded as a perfect industrial example.
Yet Nature brings her own cathartic frisson,
Now all that's left is peace.

Lisa Garside (Sherston)

Red

It holds the truth of many a lie,
Passion many burn of this hue,
But temper it shows can never be explained.
You hold the colour of perish and clarity,
It states well-being, control and ambition.
But beyond layers a natural desire to consume,
May heal a heart.
To fall into you one must be brave and a little stupid,
You may give most but demand much from your followers,
Many ignore the warning of danger lost in the passions stirred.
Mild moods collapse beyond the safe-thinking world,
The imagination is simple rhythms outside the realm of normality.
The fire of passion most suitably matches the flippant personality
of red,
Both hold the price of excitement with shortened lives metaphysical
and literal.

Ian Fisher (Taunton)

My Country Village

Our village is a pretty one
Of mellow Cotswold stone
Many people come and sit
By the river, of the Coln.

They wander here, and everywhere
No fear, as traffic drives through.
Walking backwards, cameras clicking
Taking pictures of the view.

Village people are the strangers now
Cottages have all been bought
No longer, a friendly face to greet
No one gives us a thought.

No friendly neighbour comes to call
No one has time to spare
Times have changed since I was born
In the cottage, on The Square.

O E Stringer (Cirencester)

Caught In The Headlights

alert to possibilities
a tabby cat sits motionless
unblinking eyes focused
on a well-worn burrow

. . . a young doe surfaces

fatefully, she pauses;
two haunting squeals
rend the air; then a third
diminuendo

. . . a child stirs

he drowns in dreams
and echoing screams
tumbling and spinning
like Monday's washing

. . . a mother wakes

the muscles under the soft
mound of her belly stiffen,
she waits until he settles;
alert to possibilities.

Sylvia Fairclough (Bath)

Wreckers

A cold November night - the sky inky-black;
No stars, no moon to light the way.
A gale blowing across the Atlantic Ocean,
Whipping the waves in its fury, to great heights
That break upon the shore, sending their spray
Up to the men waiting on the cliffs above the beach.
Silently waiting, waiting, waiting.

Can their luck change tonight?
Will a ship come crashing onto the rocks below,
Scattering its precious cargo into the shallows
Within reach of the cold and hungry crowd
Waiting and shivering on the sand?
Watching and listening in the bitter wind.
Anxiously waiting, waiting, waiting.

There have been no wrecks along this coast
For many weeks, supplies of food and ale are running out.
Now they are desperate, willing to risk all
To help them in their plight.
Surely their luck must change soon.
Perhaps tonight is such a night,
So they are waiting, waiting, waiting.

Then in the early hours, before the dawn,
A ship is blow onto the jagged rocks,
Its timbers smashed, its cargo tossed into the heaving waves.
'A ship! A ship!' they cry. 'Thanks be to God!'
And crates and barrels, bits of broken wood
Are rescued from the sea by many grateful hands,
No longer waiting, waiting, waiting.

Now there'll be food for the table, wood for the fire,
Ale for the drinking, new clothes for their backs
And till the next ship strikes the rocks,
No more waiting, waiting, waiting.

Ann Linney (Redruth)

Where I Belong . . .

Empty winter beach,
Ebb tide leaves mirrored pools.
Lovers stroll, hold hands.

Seabirds wheeling high,
Reach for the towering crags,
Swoop to foaming surf.

Gone the summer throng,
Stretches the endless gold sand,
Sea air fills my lungs.

Atlantic rollers curve,
White foam caresses the rocks -
Telling me, I'm home.

Alan Murton (Truro)

Home Ground

My home is in Hampshire, a most southern part
Of the British Isles, so where shall I start?
It is bordered with Wilts, Dorset, Sussex and Berks
And is home to the New Forest National Park.
I live in Southampton where the Spitfires were made
And where the Titanic sailed from before that fateful day.
Beautiful parks surround the city
Where gardeners are busy keeping them pretty.
There are acres of common for walking through
And a sports centre with a ski slope too.
Victoria Park, site of the old Netley Hospital
Where nurse Florence Nightingale worked and gave her all.
Southampton, in bygone days, a walled city had been
And there are lots of the old walls still to be seen.
Ancient and modern standing tall
History versus the new the new shopping malls.
The oldest bowling green has passed the test of time
Built in the city in twelve ninety-nine
Our churches and museums are all old timers
And the docks, old and new, play host to the liners.
The Isle of Wight sits twenty miles away
At the junction of the Solent and Spithead waterways
With The Needles, Osborne House and Alum Bay
And Carisbrooke Castle where King Charles the First stayed.
Portsmouth Docks are just along the coast
Decades of naval history they can boast
Warships and galleons to the capstans are tied
And the new Spinnaker Tower now is spied
This coastal region is as old as time
And I am proud to call this city mine.

Jan Collingwood (Southampton)

What's A Region?

Is a region a collection of buildings?
A line on a map or just a parcel of land?
Is it a space in which certain people live,
People who gain their identity from the soil
On which they stand
Or is a region, a space that we, its residents,
Are allowed to make our own?

If that's the case, what of the visitors,
Those who arrive from overseas to
Clog up our pathways
Increase the queues at the bank
And encourage shopkeepers to sell
Postcards rather than food?

My region is clogged.
My beloved city, Oxford, overrun.
Visitors walk in wriggling crocodile lines,
Taking up the space I once assumed was mine.
And I am told this is good,
That they bring prosperity to those living here.

Should this be so, what worth prosperity,
If it means that we, the residents
Have to walk in the road because the pavements
Are full?

Helen Peacocke (Oxford)

A Soft Triumphant Chorus

Yesterday had been cold and bitter,
winter lingering on the frost under the bare trees,
the wind had been a lash, the raindrops like ice.
But this morning had brought with it, the
long sweet breath of spring like a smile,
like a soft triumphant chorus hardly heard, only felt.
Never in winter had I witnessed such a sky,
so pure tinted like a robin's egg, across which
moved thin drifts of clouds, radiant before the new sun.
The brown, wet earth lay under the light, still naked,
but softened by the early mist and
exhaling a thousand strong and fertile scents
too intoxicating for endurance.
The trees were still empty, yet there was a
pliability about their branches, a gentle blurring;
no longer were they stark and hard and rigid
as they had been only yesterday.
A faint greenness like a haze touched a distant park,
when all grass had lain like rutted iron the other morning.
Dogs and cats lifted their voices excitedly as if they had
slept all winter and had come awake only at this hour.
Robins hopped over the ground, their red-umber breasts
bright in the sunlight and sparrows twittered
noisily in the eaves over the slate roof of a
church, damp from the rains of the night now flowed
like water with the blue reflection from the sky.
I felt the earth under my feet,
all at once it seemed to pulse against them
like a deep awakening heart.
I stood on the heart of the earth and I knew it was alive.

Judith McCarthy (Oxford)

Solitude . . . The Green Way

In my small piece of landscape
I can privately escape
To muse on this chequered drape.

Away from prying eyes of man
Beneath a sky hued cyan
My eyes look upwards, and scan.

A gentle breeze nuzzles by
As I reify in my mind's eye
Beside a sleepy, wispy snye.

Through this scene, mellow, tranquil
Daffodils of dainty jonquil
Shimmer and shake a delicate frill.

Ann White (Bristol)

Look Ahead

What does it matter if your hair is grey
Your face all wrinkled and looks all worn,
The sun still shines on a bright day,
And life goes on from the day you were born,
If you are able to get up in the morning
And face each day with gladness and joy,
All troubles that are there to affect you
Can fade away, to become things of the past,
With a smile and a nod to all that you meet,
Life in turn helps you to go on,
And your smile will have helped others,
To help them to respond as they go on their way,
Life is so short, so look for the best
If it's not straight ahead, it'll be round the corner,
And who knows it may be the best of all.

Phyllis Wright (Basingstoke)

Pans People In A Roundabout Way

Who said Pagan worship was on the decline
And that Stonehenge has run out of time?
You've let your guard down on these devilish mothers
Take a warning from me my tax-paying brothers

They've been sighted at midnight on Braunton's misty burrows
Doing what they do in newly ploughed furrows
Pan's People are abroad in these troubled times
Forget those stone circles we're talking ley lines

It's our elected warlocks that did this foul deed
Spending thousands of pounds, they say we don't need
Trying to take us back to our mystical past
These high priests of mammon you know the cast

Have for our frustration education and despair
Erected on the roundabout, daisy chains everywhere
Some graffiti is needed to fill in the detail
Care of a chav or a goth anything cloven foot horns and tail.

Charles Keeble (Barnstaple)

A Centenarian Remembers (1906-2006)

We were a happy family - but Father's word was law
Until he went to serve his King and country in the war.
A struggle it became for Mum with six of us to feed:
We soon were taught the difference between a want and need.

We entertained ourselves before the advent of TV,
A cardboard box across the floor was like a ship at sea.
We often had our arguments and sometimes we would fight
And yet we knew, instinctively, to discard wrong for right.

At home, at school, at Sunday school, they all had this to say:
'Do not put off until next week what can be done today.'
Our father came home wounded, spent many years in bed;
Our life was tough, yet discipline had stood us in good stead.

We all made happy marriages, established good careers,
Becoming useful citizens throughout ensuing years.
I wonder if the young today are going to survive
With problems of obesity which start at age of five.

They will abuse the Internet, get hooked on drugs and drink;
If only they would give themselves the time to stop and think!
We were content with what we had; we did not carry knives.
Old-fashioned values, if applied, may yet enhance young lives.

Graham Winterbourne (Uffculme)

Minehead Mourning

So! He is gone? That must be right,
For he has not come back.
We were together when he breathed his last.
It only took one day to bring this aching lack.

One day! The day before, a man at peace
With evening light, not known till these last years.
He was still strong, older yes, but strong
With plans for garden, friends and not for tears.

He always was so thankful for each day,
To look upon our hills and town below,
And see the valleys or neat marshes and the bay;
Days to see the trains come in and go.

May I not leave this place of peace
Where we have shared our life, our work, our thoughts;
Not drift like silt downhill to valley floor
To craggy-fastness flats and safer courts.

I see the town as he did, rosemary-tiled;
The Channel's east horizon, borage-blue;
Or sit and weep on lawns where we once smiled;
Or see the sea's now fudge-brown, mud-brown brew.

Come! Come! For love is here and lives on still
In those who loved him - family and friends
Between each bolstering high-rise hill
There's memory of him and love that never ends.

E M Parbrook (Minehead)

Britain

This Britain, our homeland, the land we adore,
Its beauty surrounds us from mountain to moor.
Forests and rivers, land fertile and green,
Fauna and flora to enjoy and be seen.
Ancient cathedrals and monuments tall,
Historic castles, our heritage all.
We have freedom to speak, travel and pray
Thanking God for our country and life here today.
Also for those we choose to elect
To rule in our name, the Queen we respect.
Let us extend warm and friendly hands
To new settlers from foreign lands.
They hope to find a better life
Enrich us with their culture, from hatred and strife.
From our aggressors they will help to defend
These British Isles, to be a friend,
Preserve our peaceful way of living,
Each one taking, each one giving,
Bring Britons closer, whatever the miles,
Sharing our pride in these British Isles.

Patricia Evans (Exeter)

Terminal

No more lying in bed for me
Now it's my turn to make the tea
Fetch the shopping, pay a bill
These you did before you were ill

You took over the cooking when you retired
Producing lovely meals that were much admired
Sadly, you no longer have an appetite
So I make do, with something light

The garden is getting very overgrown
By now you would have the spring seeds sown
The grass is too long, the hedge needs trimming
There's so much to do my head is spinning

No more trips to the country or the seaside
Now it's ambulances take us for a ride
Nurses and doctors are caring for you
It seems there is no more that I can do

I hope and pray it is not too late
To tell you how much I appreciate
The care you have shown me all these years
Forgive me dear if I can't stay my tears

Beryl Miles (Letchworth Garden City)

Forward Press Information

We hope you have enjoyed reading this book - and that you will continue to enjoy it in the coming years.

If you like reading and writing poetry drop us a line, or give us a call, and we'll send you a free information pack.

Alternatively if you would like to order further copies of this book or any of our other titles, then please give us a call or log onto our website at www.forwardpress.co.uk

Forward Press Ltd. Information
Remus House
Coltsfoot Drive
Peterborough
PE2 9JX

(01733) 898101